RISING ★ STARS

New Curriculum
Arithmetic Practice Tests

YEAR 3

Louise Moore and Cherri Moseley

ISBN: 978 1 4718 9383 4
Text, design and layout © Rising Stars UK Ltd 2017
First published in 2017 by Rising Stars UK Ltd
Rising Stars UK Ltd, part of Hodder Education Group,
An Hachette UK Company
Carmelite House, 50 Victoria Embankment, London, EC4Y 0DZ
www.risingstars-uk.com
All facts are correct at time of going to press.

Authors: Louise Moore and Cherri Moseley
Publisher: Kate Baxter
Editorial: Out of House Publishing
Cover design: Burville-Riley Partnership
Illustrations by Newgen
Printed by: Ashford Colour Press Ltd

A catalogue record for this title is available from the British Library.

Contents

Introduction

Arithmetic skills

Arithmetic is an important life skill and regular practice is critical. Without fluency in mental arithmetic to underpin their work in numbers, children will struggle with many other areas of mathematics. Children who are fluent with number and place value will be able to use their skills to find efficient strategies for completing calculations by recalling and applying number knowledge rapidly and accurately. They will also be able to reason through derived facts, e.g. knowing that $50 \times 70 = 3500$ through knowledge of $5 \times 7 = 35$.

The National Tests

From May 2016, the end-of-Key-Stage Mathematics Tests have assessed children to ascertain what they have achieved in relation to the statements outlined in the 2014 Mathematics Programmes of Study. The mathematics tests comprise two components presented as two separate tests at Key Stage 1 and three separate tests at Key Stage 2. The first of these tests, in both Key Stages, is an arithmetic test. The use of calculators is not permitted. It is important to introduce the practice of arithmetic skills early and provide regular opportunities to embed them, starting with shorter tests and building to the number of questions/time allowed for each test gradually.

The questions in the arithmetic test paper are presented as context-free calculations for constructed responses. There is no time limit for the end of Key Stage 1 test, but the end-of-Key-Stage 2 test has a time limit of 30 minutes. There is one mark awarded for a correct response to the majority of arithmetic calculations. However, some questions may be awarded two marks where the formal method of working may gain one mark if the answer is incorrect.

Overall success in the National Test for Arithmetic relies on being able to complete at least one question per minute on average at the end of Key Stage 2. To achieve this, reliable and efficient arithmetic skills are essential. Children should therefore be encouraged to develop good mental arithmetic skills wherever this is appropriate.

This series provides opportunities for children to build their fluency and enables them to become familiar with completing arithmetic questions quickly under test conditions.

Skills and knowledge covered in this set of tests:

- Count from 0 in multiples of 4, 8, 50 and 100 [3N1b]
- Find 10 or 100 more or less than a given number [3N2b]
- Add and subtract mentally [3C1]
- Add and subtract using formal written methods of columnar addition and subtraction [3C2]
- Solve addition and subtraction problems including missing numbers [3C4]
- Recall multiplication and division facts for the 3, 4 and 8 multiplication tables [3C6]
- Calculate multiplication and division statements mentally and using formal written methods [3C7]
- Solve multiplication and division problems including missing numbers [3C8]
- Count up and down in tenths [3F1a]
- Find fractions of a discrete set of objects [3F1b]
- Add and subtract fractions with the same denominator [3F4]

How to use this book

Aim of these books

The aim of this series of Arithmetic Practice Tests is to provide material that will support children to gain proficiency in arithmetic in order to meet or exceed the expectations of the New National Curriculum in England (2014). For some children, it may be necessary to use content from the book for the year below their actual school year if skills have not yet been mastered. It is recommended that the majority of children move through the programme of study at broadly the same pace. However, children who are not sufficiently fluent should be provided with extra practice to consolidate their skills.

The books in the Arithmetic Practice Tests Set A series provide practice opportunities with built-in progression. Each test in the Arithmetic Practice Tests Set B series includes content from across the arithmetic objectives in the National Curriculum (2014) for the relevant year group. These can be used alongside the more progressive tests in the first set of books, or progress through the first set can be accelerated and the tests in the second set used as preparation for assessment in the second half of the year. This flexibility allows teachers to use the combination of books to meet the particular needs of the children in their class. For each test, in both sets of books, there is a built-in facility to analyse test results to help teachers identify where children are secure or have gaps in their knowledge.

Skills used in the tests

The tests in this book include all the arithmetic skills indicated in the National Curriculum in England (2014) for Year 3. The skills used in each test are listed in the contents and on the teacher's page. There is some overlap between the years, and this is indicated in each test by references to the content domain.

Teaching suggestions

For each test in Arithmetic Practice Tests Set B, a focus activity is suggested, which teachers may choose to use to introduce or consolidate a skill encountered in the test. Where the school has a policy for how arithmetic is taught, teachers should adhere to the school policy to avoid confusion.

Some of the tests could be completed as a paired activity, allowing collaborative working and learning as well as test-based activities. It is also useful to mark the tests with the children, allowing time to discuss successful methods and common misconceptions.

Structure of the tests

Questions are given in a general order of difficulty, though since different children find certain concepts more difficult from others, some may find later questions easier than earlier ones. Some questions are set out to encourage formal methods of working. Six tests are presented for each of three terms, although the tests can be administered at any time at the teacher's discretion. Using all the tests from Sets A and B will provide enough practice for one test a week. The number of questions increases while the time allowed to complete each test decreases each term and in each year. The final tests in Year 6 provide 40 marks within a 30-minute timeframe to equate to a full SATS practice test.

Assessment grid

At the end of each test an assessment grid appears. After the tests have been marked, the children can be asked, 'How well did you do?' and encouraged to colour the numbers of the questions they completed correctly. Most question numbers appear more than once in the grid. This is to extend its usefulness as a diagnostic tool. At a quick glance, the teacher can assess which children need further teaching in specific areas of arithmetic.

The following abbreviations are used throughout:

Abbreviation	Meaning
O	numbers that only have ones
T	numbers that only have tens
TO	numbers that have tens and ones
HTO	numbers that have hundreds, tens and ones
$+, -, \times, \div$	for the relevant operation
$\pm$	to show numbers can be added or subtracted

Administering the tests

In the Year 3 book, there is a recommended time limited of 25 minutes per test.

Mark scheme

The majority of the questions in the Arithmetic Practice Tests are allocated one mark. Questions should be marked correct or incorrect, in line with the National Tests marking scheme; half marks are not allowed. Where two marks are available for a question, this indicates that a particular written method may be awarded a mark even if the answer is incorrect.

Teacher guidance

A page of teacher guidance is provided to support each test.

Skills and knowledge needed for this test
The key skills and knowledge from the current curriculum year, needed to complete the test, are listed. Skills from previous year levels are assumed to have been mastered.

Timing
The number of minutes allowed for each test is indicated.

Focus activity
Ideas for ways to review previous skills/knowledge or introduce new skills are provided. It is advised that these are taught and children are given time to practise before the test is administered.

Answers
Answers to all questions in the test are provided in the grid.

Marks
The number of marks allocated to each questions is indicated in the grid.

Related focus activities
Focus activities in which similar skills are taught are indicated for each question. If children get a particular question incorrect, the listed focus activities and accompanying test questions can be revisited to provide further practice at an easier level to build skills and confidence.

Autumn Test 1
Teacher guidance

Skills and knowledge covered in this test:
- Count from 0 in multiples of 4, 8, 50 and 100 [3N1b]
- Find 10 or 100 more or less than a given number [3N2b]
- Add and subtract mentally [3C1]
- Add and subtract using formal written methods of columnar addition and subtraction [3C2]
- Solve addition and subtraction problems including missing numbers [3C4]
- Recall multiplication and division facts for the 3, 4 and 8 multiplication tables [3C6]
- Calculate multiplication and division statements mentally and using formal written methods [3C7]
- Solve multiplication and division problems including missing numbers [3C8]
- Count up and down in tenths [3F1a]
- Find fractions of a discrete set of objects [3F1b]
- Add and subtract fractions with the same denominator [3F4]

Focus activity: Additive place value

3C1

You will need: place-value cards.

Step 1 There are at least three different aspects to place value. These are rarely made explicit to children. You could explain simply:

Positional is the position that the digit is placed in, e.g. does the digit 7, in 475, represent the ones, tens or hundreds?

Multiplicative is when the digit is multiplied by its positional value to give its true value, e.g. in the number 475, the true value of the 7 is 70.

Additive is when we add together the true value of each digit to give the whole number, e.g. 475 is 400 + 70 + 5.

Step 2 Focus on the additive aspect of place value. Give children sets of hundreds, tens and ones place-value cards. Ask them to make nine different 3-digit numbers, using each number once. Children record each of their numbers by showing the addition of the parts, e.g. 500 + 20 + 9 = 529.

Step 3 Challenge children to order the nine numbers they have made from smallest to largest. They only need to look at the hundreds digit since there can only be one number with each hundreds value.

Qu. No.	Question	Answer	Mark	Domain ref.	Focus activity
1	5 + 3 = □	8	1	1C1	Y1 Autumn Test 2, Y1 Summer Test 4
2	6 − □ = 4	2	1	1C4	Y1 Spring Test 1, Y1 Spring Test 5, Y1 Summer Test 4, Y1 Summer Test 6
3	2 × 6 = □	12	1	2C6	Y2 Spring Test 1, Y2 Spring Test 2
4	15 − 8 = □	7	1	2C1	Y1 Summer Test 3, Y1 Summer Test 4
5	50 + 10 + 10 = □	70	1	2N1	Y2 Autumn Test 5
6	26 + □ = 29	3	1	2C2a, 2C2b	Y2 Autumn Test 1, Y2 Summer Test 5
7	60 ÷ 10 = □	6	1	2C6	Y2 Spring Test 3, Y2 Spring Test 4, Y2 Spring Test 5, Y2 Spring Test 6
8	46 + 50 = □	96	1	2C2a, 2C2b	Y2 Autumn Test 5
9	□ = 3 + 6 + 7	16	1	2C2a, 2C2b	Y2 Autumn Test 4
10	½ of 10 = □	5	1	2F1a	Y2 Summer Test 3
11	92 − 26 = □	66	1	2C2a, 2C2b	Y2 Summer Test 2, Y2 Summer Test 4
12	⅓ of 9 = □	3	1	2F1a	Y2 Summer Test 3
13	146 − 10 = □	136	1	3N2b	Y3 Autumn Test 3
14	295 + 4 = □	299	1	3C1	Y3 Autumn Test 2
15	374 + 284 = □	658	1	3C2	Y3 Autumn Test 4
16	8 × 2 = □	16	1	3C6	Y3 Spring Test 5
17	675 − 30 = □	645	1	3C1	Y3 Autumn Test 3
18	3 × 4 = □	12	1	3C6	Y3 Spring Test 3, Y3 Spring Test 5
19	□ = 675 − 435	240	1	3C2	Y3 Summer Test 1
20	1/10 + 2/10 = □	4/10	1	3F1a	Y3 Autumn Test 4, Y3 Spring Test 1
21	□ + 431 = 643	212	1	3C4	Y3 Autumn Test 4, Y3 Summer Test 6
22	1/5 + 3/5 = □	4/5	1	3F4	Y3 Autumn Test 5
23	□ ÷ 8 = 2	16	1	3C8	Y3 Summer Test 4, Y3 Summer Test 6
24	32 × 4 = □	128	1	3C7	Y3 Spring Test 6, Y3 Summer Test 5
25	⅛ of 16 = □	2	1	3F1b	Y3 Summer Test 3

Arithmetic Practice Tests Set B Year 3 © Rising Stars UK Ltd 2017   11

Photocopiable tests

Each test comprises two pages to be photocopied for each child.

Test first page features

Question numbers are clearly shown.

Space is provided for children to write their names, class and the date the test is taken.

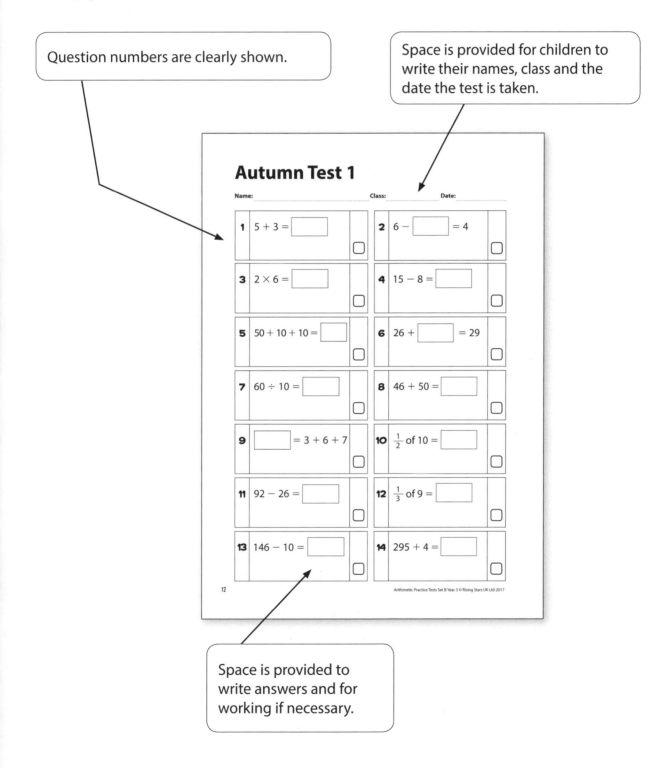

Autumn Test 1

Name: _____ Class: _____ Date: _____

1 $5 + 3 =$ ⬜	**2** $6 - $ ⬜ $= 4$
3 $2 \times 6 =$ ⬜	**4** $15 - 8 =$ ⬜
5 $50 + 10 + 10 =$ ⬜	**6** $26 + $ ⬜ $= 29$
7 $60 \div 10 =$ ⬜	**8** $46 + 50 =$ ⬜
9 ⬜ $= 3 + 6 + 7$	**10** $\frac{1}{2}$ of $10 =$ ⬜
11 $92 - 26 =$ ⬜	**12** $\frac{1}{3}$ of $9 =$ ⬜
13 $146 - 10 =$ ⬜	**14** $295 + 4 =$ ⬜

12

Arithmetic Practice Tests Set B Year 3 © Rising Stars UK Ltd 2017

Space is provided to write answers and for working if necessary.

Photocopiable tests (continued)

Each test comprises two pages to be photocopied for each child.

Test second page features

Marks for each question can be written in the score boxes.

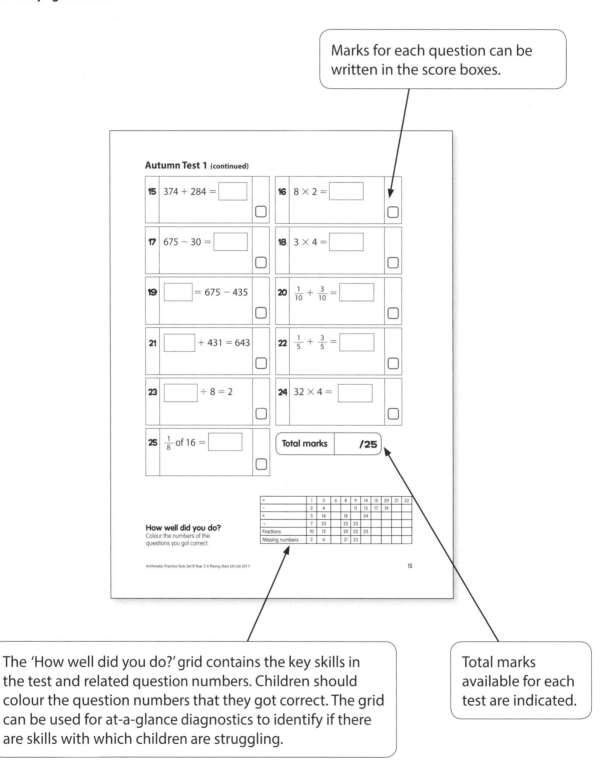

The 'How well did you do?' grid contains the key skills in the test and related question numbers. Children should colour the question numbers that they got correct. The grid can be used for at-a-glance diagnostics to identify if there are skills with which children are struggling.

Total marks available for each test are indicated.

Autumn Test 1

Teacher guidance

Skills and knowledge covered in this test:

- Count from 0 in multiples of 4, 8, 50 and 100 [3N1b]
- Find 10 or 100 more or less than a given number [3N2b]
- Add and subtract mentally [3C1]
- Add and subtract using formal written methods of columnar addition and subtraction [3C2]
- Solve addition and subtraction problems including missing numbers [3C4]
- Recall multiplication and division facts for the 3, 4 and 8 multiplication tables [3C6]
- Calculate multiplication and division statements mentally and using formal written methods [3C7]
- Solve multiplication and division problems including missing numbers [3C8]
- Count up and down in tenths [3F1a]
- Find fractions of a discrete set of objects [3F1b]
- Add and subtract fractions with the same denominator [3F4]

Focus activity: Additive place value

3C1

You will need: place-value cards.

 There are at least three different aspects to place value. These are rarely made explicit to children. You could explain simply:

Positional is the position that the digit is placed in, e.g. does the digit 7, in 475, represent the ones, tens or hundreds?

Multiplicative is when the digit is multiplied by its positional value to give its true value, e.g. in the number 475, the true value of the 7 is 70.

Additive is when we add together the true value of each digit to give the whole number, e.g. 475 is 400 + 70 + 5.

 Focus on the additive aspect of place value. Give children sets of hundreds, tens and ones place-value cards. Ask them to make nine different 3-digit numbers, using each number once. Children record each of their numbers by showing the addition of the parts, e.g. 500 + 20 + 9 = 529.

 Challenge children to order the nine numbers they have made from smallest to largest. They only need to look at the hundreds digit since there can only be one number with each hundreds value.

Qu. No.	Question	Answer	Mark	Domain ref.	Focus activity
1	$5 + 3 = \square$	8	1	1C1	Y1 Autumn Test 2, Y1 Summer Test 4
2	$6 - \square = 4$	2	1	1C4	Y1 Spring Test 1, Y1 Spring Test 5, Y1 Summer Test 4, Y1 Summer Test 6
3	$2 \times 6 = \square$	12	1	2C6	Y2 Spring Test 1, Y2 Spring Test 2
4	$15 - 8 = \square$	7	1	2C1	Y1 Summer Test 3, Y1 Summer Test 4
5	$50 + 10 + 10 = \square$	70	1	2N1	Y2 Autumn Test 5
6	$26 + \square = 29$	3	1	2C2a, 2C2b	Y2 Autumn Test 1, Y2 Summer Test 5
7	$60 \div 10 = \square$	6	1	2C6	Y2 Spring Test 3, Y2 Spring Test 4, Y2 Spring Test 5, Y2 Spring Test 6
8	$46 + 50 = \square$	96	1	2C2a, 2C2b	Y2 Autumn Test 5
9	$\square = 3 + 6 + 7$	16	1	2C2a, 2C2b	Y2 Autumn Test 4
10	$\frac{1}{2}$ of $10 = \square$	5	1	2F1a	Y2 Summer Test 3
11	$92 - 26 = \square$	66	1	2C2a, 2C2b	Y2 Summer Test 2, Y2 Summer Test 4
12	$\frac{1}{3}$ of $9 = \square$	3	1	2F1a	Y2 Summer Test 3
13	$146 - 10 = \square$	136	1	3N2b	Y3 Autumn Test 3
14	$295 + 4 = \square$	299	1	3C1	Y3 Autumn Test 2
15	$374 + 284 = \square$	658	1	3C2	Y3 Autumn Test 4
16	$8 \times 2 = \square$	16	1	3C6	Y3 Spring Test 5
17	$675 - 30 = \square$	645	1	3C1	Y3 Autumn Test 3
18	$3 \times 4 = \square$	12	1	3C6	Y3 Spring Test 3, Y3 Spring Test 5
19	$\square = 675 - 435$	240	1	3C2	Y3 Summer Test 1
20	$\frac{1}{10} + \frac{3}{10} = \square$	$\frac{4}{10}$	1	3F1a	Y3 Autumn Test 5, Y3 Spring Test 1
21	$\square + 431 = 643$	212	1	3C4	Y3 Autumn Test 4, Y3 Summer Test 6
22	$\frac{1}{5} + \frac{3}{5} = \square$	$\frac{4}{5}$	1	3F4	Y3 Autumn Test 5
23	$\square \div 8 = 2$	16	1	3C8	Y3 Spring Test 4, Y3 Summer Test 6
24	$32 \times 4 = \square$	128	1	3C7	Y3 Spring Test 6, Y3 Summer Test 5
25	$\frac{1}{8}$ of $16 = \square$	2	1	3F1b	Y3 Summer Test 3

Autumn Test 1

Name: .... **Class:** .... **Date:** ....

1 $5 + 3 = $ ⬚

2 $6 - $ ⬚ $= 4$

3 $2 \times 6 = $ ⬚

4 $15 - 8 = $ ⬚

5 $50 + 10 + 10 = $ ⬚

6 $26 + $ ⬚ $= 29$

7 $60 \div 10 = $ ⬚

8 $46 + 50 = $ ⬚

9 ⬚ $= 3 + 6 + 7$

10 $\frac{1}{2}$ of $10 = $ ⬚

11 $92 - 26 = $ ⬚

12 $\frac{1}{3}$ of $9 = $ ⬚

13 $146 - 10 = $ ⬚

14 $295 + 4 = $ ⬚

Arithmetic Practice Tests Set B Year 3 © Rising Stars UK Ltd 2017

Autumn Test 1 (continued)

15 $374 + 284 =$ ☐ ☐

16 $8 \times 2 =$ ☐ ☐

17 $675 - 30 =$ ☐ ☐

18 $3 \times 4 =$ ☐ ☐

19 ☐ $= 675 - 435$ ☐

20 $\dfrac{1}{10} + \dfrac{3}{10} =$ ☐ ☐

21 ☐ $+ 431 = 643$ ☐

22 $\dfrac{1}{5} + \dfrac{3}{5} =$ ☐ ☐

23 ☐ $\div 8 = 2$ ☐

24 $32 \times 4 =$ ☐ ☐

25 $\dfrac{1}{8}$ of $16 =$ ☐ ☐

Total marks	/25

How well did you do?
Colour the numbers of the questions you got correct.

+	1	5	6	8	9	14	15	20	21	22
−	2	4			11	13	17	19		
×	3	16		18		24				
÷	7	23		23	23					
Fractions	10	12		20	22	25				
Missing numbers	2	6		21	23					

Autumn Test 2

Teacher guidance

25 minutes

Skills and knowledge covered in this test:

- Count from 0 in multiples of 4, 8, 50 and 100 [3N1b]
- Find 10 or 100 more or less than a given number [3N2b]
- Add and subtract mentally [3C1]
- Add and subtract using formal written methods of columnar addition and subtraction [3C2]
- Solve addition and subtraction problems including missing numbers [3C4]
- Recall multiplication and division facts for the 3, 4 and 8 multiplication tables [3C6]
- Calculate multiplication and division statements mentally and using formal written methods [3C7]
- Solve multiplication and division problems including missing numbers [3C8]
- Count up and down in tenths [3F1a]
- Find fractions of a discrete set of objects [3F1b]
- Add and subtract fractions with the same denominator [3F4]

Focus activity: Adding or subtracting a single-digit number and a 3-digit number mentally

3C1

You will need: place-value cards.

 Step 1 Make a 3-digit number with place-value cards. Use the cards to talk about the value of each digit.

 Step 2 Choose a further single-digit place-value card. Ask children to suggest ways to add this number to your 3-digit number. List the suggestions. Explore subtraction in the same way. Methods are likely to include:

Addition	Subtraction
Count on, with or without a number line.	Count back, with or without a number line.
Use number bonds to 10, near bonds, doubles or near doubles.	Partition the 3-digit number, including one ten in the smaller part of the number, e.g. 357 → 340 + 17. Subtract the single-digit number from 17, adding the difference to 340.
Add and subtract the difference between the single-digit number and 10, e.g. 357 + 8 = 357 + 10 − 2 = 367 − 2 = 365.	Subtract 10 and add the difference between the single-digit number and 10, e.g. 357 − 8 = 357 − 10 + 2 = 347 + 2 = 349.

 Step 3 Choose a different single-digit number to add and subtract to your 3-digit number. Check that each method can still be used. Add any additional methods to your lists.

 Step 4 Display the lists. Encourage children to try a different method.

Qu. No.	Question	Answer	Mark	Domain ref.	Focus activity
1	$4 + 5 = \square$	9	1	1C1	Y1 Autumn Test 2, Y1 Summer Test 4
2	$3 - \square = 1$	2	1	1C4	Y1 Spring Test 1, Y1 Spring Test 5, Y1 Summer Test 4, Y1 Summer Test 6
3	$30 + 10 + 10 = \square$	50	1	2N1	Y2 Autumn Test 5
4	$10 \div 2 = \square$	5	1	2C6	Y2 Spring Test 3, Y2 Spring Test 4, Y2 Spring Test 5, Y2 Spring Test 6
5	$4 \times 5 = \square$	20	1	2C6	Y2 Spring Test 1, Y2 Spring Test 2
6	$\square = 17 - 9$	8	1	2C1	Y1 Summer Test 3, Y1 Summer Test 4
7	$42 - 3 = \square$	39	1	2C2a, 2C2b	Y2 Autumn Test 2
8	$5 + 2 + 8 = \square$	15	1	2C2a, 2C2b	Y2 Autumn Test 4
9	$38 + 10 = \square$	48	1	3N2b	Y2 Autumn Test 5
10	$73 - 20 = \square$	53	1	2C2a, 2C2b	Y2 Autumn Test 5
11	$\frac{1}{3}$ of 6 = $\square$	2	1	2F1a	Y2 Summer Test 3
12	$534 - 5 = \square$	529	1	3C1	Y3 Autumn Test 2
13	$\frac{1}{4}$ of 8 = $\square$	2	1	2F1a	Y2 Summer Test 3
14	$72 - 19 = \square$	53	1	2C2a, 2C2b	Y2 Summer Test 2, Y2 Summer Test 4
15	$4 \times 6 = \square$	24	1	3C6	Y3 Spring Test 5
16	$265 + \square = 677$	412	1	3C4	Y3 Autumn Test 4, Y3 Summer Test 6
17	$843 + 50 = \square$	893	1	3C1	Y3 Autumn Test 3
18	$584 - 257 = \square$	327	1	3C2	Y3 Summer Test 1
19	$376 + 8 = \square$	384	1	3C1	Y3 Autumn Test 2
20	$3 \times \square = 12$	4	1	3C8	Y3 Spring Test 4, Y3 Summer Test 6
21	$\square = 394 + 412$	806	1	3C2	Y3 Autumn Test 4
22	$\frac{2}{10} + \frac{7}{10} = \square$	$\frac{9}{10}$	1	3F1a	Y3 Autumn Test 5, Y3 Spring Test 1
23	$45 \times 3 = \square$	135	1	3C7	Y3 Spring Test 6, Y3 Summer Test 5
24	$\frac{1}{6} + \frac{4}{6} = \square$	$\frac{5}{6}$	1	3F4	Y3 Autumn Test 5
25	$\frac{1}{5}$ of 15 = $\square$	3	1	3F1b	Y3 Summer Test 3

Autumn Test 2

Name: ....   **Class:** ....   **Date:** ....

1 | $4 + 5 = \boxed{}$

2 | $3 - \boxed{} = 1$

3 | $30 + 10 + 10 = \boxed{}$

4 | $10 \div 2 = \boxed{}$

5 | $4 \times 5 = \boxed{}$

6 | $\boxed{} = 17 - 9$

7 | $42 - 3 = \boxed{}$

8 | $5 + 2 + 8 = \boxed{}$

9 | $38 + 10 = \boxed{}$

10 | $73 - 20 = \boxed{}$

11 | $\frac{1}{3}$ of $6 = \boxed{}$

12 | $534 - 5 = \boxed{}$

13 | $\frac{1}{4}$ of $8 = \boxed{}$

14 | $72 - 19 = \boxed{}$

Autumn Test 2 (continued)

15 $4 \times 6 = \boxed{}$

16 $265 + \boxed{} = 677$

17 $843 + 50 = \boxed{}$

18 $584 - 257 = \boxed{}$

19 $376 + 8 = \boxed{}$

20 $3 \times \boxed{} = 12$

21 $\boxed{} = 394 + 412$

22 $\dfrac{2}{10} + \dfrac{7}{10} = \boxed{}$

23 $45 \times 3 = \boxed{}$

24 $\dfrac{1}{6} + \dfrac{4}{6} = \boxed{}$

25 $\dfrac{1}{5}$ of $15 = \boxed{}$

Total marks	/25

How well did you do?
Colour the numbers of the questions you got correct.

+	1	3	8	9	16	17	19	21	22	24
–	2	6	7	10		12	14		18	
x	5	15	20	23						
÷	4									
Fractions	11	13	22	24		25				
Missing numbers	2	16	20							

Arithmetic Practice Tests Set B Year 3 © Rising Stars UK Ltd 2017

Autumn Test 3

Teacher guidance

Skills and knowledge covered in this test:

- Count from 0 in multiples of 4, 8, 50 and 100 [3N1b]
- Find 10 or 100 more or less than a given number [3N2b]
- Add and subtract mentally [3C1]
- Add and subtract using formal written methods of columnar addition and subtraction [3C2]
- Solve addition and subtraction problems including missing numbers [3C4]
- Recall multiplication and division facts for the 3, 4 and 8 multiplication tables [3C6]
- Calculate multiplication and division statements mentally and using formal written methods [3C7]
- Solve multiplication and division problems including missing numbers [3C8]
- Count up and down in tenths [3F1a]
- Find fractions of a discrete set of objects [3F1b]
- Add and subtract fractions with the same denominator [3F4]

Focus activity: Adding tens or hundreds to a 3-digit number mentally

3N2b, 3C1

You will need: place-value cards.

 Make a 3-digit number with place-value cards. Use the cards to talk about the value of each digit.

 Follow the same method as the Autumn Test 2 activity, making a list of methods to add and subtract tens or hundreds. Explore how the lists for ones, tens and hundreds are very similar. Counting on or back from the appropriate digit will be in all the lists. Using number bonds and rounding with adjusting are also likely to be on each list, along with partitioning and sequencing. You may have other methods featured in your school's calculation policy.

 Children work in pairs. Give each pair a set of place-value cards. One child makes a 3-digit number. Their partner chooses a hundreds, tens or ones card for them to add or subtract. Both children calculate mentally and compare solutions and methods. Challenge each pair to use all the listed methods during the course of the activity.

 Display the lists of methods and regularly challenge children to use a particular method.

Qu. No.	Question	Answer	Mark	Domain ref.	Focus activity
1	$8 - 2 = \square$	6	1	1C1	Y1 Autumn Test 4, Y1 Summer Test 4
2	$6 \times 10 = \square$	60	1	2C6	Y2 Spring Test 1, Y2 Spring Test 2
3	$12 - 3 = \square$	9	1	2C1	Y1 Summer Test 3, Y1 Summer Test 4
4	$8 - \square = 3$	5	1	1C4	Y1 Spring Test 1, Y1 Spring Test 5, Y1 Summer Test 4, Y1 Summer Test 6
5	$8 + 5 + 5 = \square$	18	1	2C2a, 2C2b	Y2 Autumn Test 4
6	$54 + 5 = \square$	59	1	2C2a, 2C2b	Y2 Autumn Test 1
7	$\frac{1}{2}$ of $14 = \square$	7	1	2F1a	Y2 Summer Test 3
8	$\square = 80 - 10 - 10$	60	1	2N1	Y2 Autumn Test 5
9	$35 \div 5 = \square$	7	1	2C6	Y2 Spring Test 3, Y2 Spring Test 4, Y2 Spring Test 5, Y2 Spring Test 6
10	$400 - 100 = \square$	300	1	3N2b	Y3 Autumn Test 3
11	$183 - 7 = \square$	176	1	3C1	Y3 Autumn Test 2
12	$57 + 30 = \square$	87	1	2C2a, 2C2b	Y2 Autumn Test 5
13	$107 + 50 + 50 = \square$	207	1	3N1b	Y3 Autumn Test 3
14	$328 + 200 = \square$	528	1	3C1	Y3 Autumn Test 3
15	$4 \times 5 = \square$	20	1	3C6	Y3 Spring Test 3, Y3 Spring Test 5
16	$\frac{8}{10} - \frac{3}{10} = \square$	$\frac{5}{10}$	1	3F1a	Y3 Autumn Test 5, Y3 Spring Test 1
17	$8 \times 3 = \square$	24	1	3C6	Y3 Spring Test 3, Y3 Spring Test 5
18	$\frac{3}{4}$ of $8 = \square$	6	1	2F1a	Y2 Summer Test 3
19	$\square = 3 \div 10$	0.3	1	3F1a	Y3 Spring Test 1
20	$743 + 186 = \square$	929	1	3C2	Y3 Autumn Test 4
21	$\square \times 3 = 24$	8	1	3C8	Y3 Spring Test 4, Y3 Summer Test 6
22	$783 - 392 = \square$	391	1	3C2	Y3 Summer Test 1
23	$\frac{2}{3} - \frac{1}{3} = \square$	$\frac{1}{3}$	1	3F4	Y3 Autumn Test 5
24	$28 \times 5 = \square$	140	1	3C7	Y3 Spring Test 6, Y3 Summer Test 5
25	$\square - 233 = 515$	748	1	3C4	Y3 Autumn Test 4, Y3 Summer Test 6

Autumn Test 3

Name: .... **Class:** .... **Date:** ....

1 $8 - 2 = $ ☐

2 $6 \times 10 = $ ☐

3 $12 - 3 = $ ☐

4 $8 - \boxed{} = 3$ ☐

5 $8 + 5 + 5 = $ ☐

6 $54 + 5 = $ ☐

7 $\frac{1}{2}$ of $14 = $ ☐

8 $\boxed{} = 80 - 10 - 10$ ☐

9 $35 \div 5 = $ ☐

10 $400 - 100 = $ ☐

11 $183 - 7 = $ ☐

12 $57 + 30 = $ ☐

13 $107 + 50 + 50 = $ ☐

14 $328 + 200 = $ ☐

Arithmetic Practice Tests Set B Year 3 © Rising Stars UK Ltd 2017

Autumn Test 3 (continued)

15 $4 \times 5 = \boxed{}$ ☐

16 $\frac{8}{10} - \frac{3}{10} = \boxed{}$ ☐

17 $8 \times 3 = \boxed{}$ ☐

18 $\frac{3}{4}$ of $8 = \boxed{}$ ☐

19 $\boxed{} = 3 \div 10$ ☐

20 $743 + 186 = \boxed{}$ ☐

21 $\boxed{} \times 3 = 24$ ☐

22 $783 - 392 = \boxed{}$ ☐

23 $\frac{2}{3} - \frac{1}{3} = \boxed{}$ ☐

24 $28 \times 5 = \boxed{}$ ☐

25 $\boxed{} - 233 = 515$ ☐

Total marks **/25**

How well did you do?
Colour the numbers of the questions you got correct.

+		5	6	12	13	14	20				
−		1	3	4	8	10	11	16	22	23	25
×		2	15	17	21	24					
÷			9								
Fractions		7	16	18	19	23					
Missing numbers		4	21	25							

Autumn Test 4

Teacher guidance

25 minutes

Skills and knowledge covered in this test:

- Count from 0 in multiples of 4, 8, 50 and 100 [3N1b]
- Find 10 or 100 more or less than a given number [3N2b]
- Add and subtract mentally [3C1]
- Add and subtract using formal written methods of columnar addition and subtraction [3C2]
- Solve addition and subtraction problems including missing numbers [3C4]
- Recall multiplication and division facts for the 3, 4 and 8 multiplication tables [3C6]

- Calculate multiplication and division statements mentally and using formal written methods [3C7]
- Solve multiplication and division problems including missing numbers [3C8]
- Count up and down in tenths [3F1a]
- Find fractions of a discrete set of objects [3F1b]
- Add and subtract fractions with the same denominator [3F4]

Focus activity: Developing written methods for adding two 3-digit numbers

3C2, 3C4

You will need: Base 10 apparatus, place-value cards.

 Step 1 Make two 3-digit number using Base 10 apparatus. Make the same numbers with place-value cards.

 Step 2 Place the 3-digit numbers, one below the other, using the place-value cards.

$$436$$
$$+ 148$$

 Step 3 Add the hundreds flats together, recording them on the next line. Then add the ten sticks together, recording this on the next line. Now add the ones cubes together and record on the next line. Check each addition by removing the relevant place-value cards from both numbers and adding them mentally. Finally, add the three numbers together to find the sum.

$$436$$
$$+ 148$$

$$\begin{array}{r} 500 \\ 70 \\ 14 \\ \hline 584 \end{array}$$

 Step 4 When children are confident with the vertical partitioning method, introduce the short written method, continuing to use apparatus. Add the ones, exchanging ten ones for one ten. Mark this in the tens column. Exchange ten tens for one hundred where necessary. Follow the guidance in your school calculation policy on where to record this exchange.

$$436$$
$$+ 148$$
$$\overline{584}$$

Qu. No.	Question	Answer	Mark	Domain ref.	Focus activity
1	$7 - 6 = \square$	1	1	1C1	Y1 Autumn Test 4, Y1 Summer Test 4
2	$9 - \square = 9$	0	1	1C4	Y1 Autumn Test 4, Y1 Spring Test 5, Y1 Spring Test 6, Y1 Summer Test 4
3	$40 - 10 - 10 = \square$	20	1	2N1	Y2 Autumn Test 5
4	$8 \div 2 = \square$	4	1	2C6	Y2 Spring Test 3, Y2 Spring Test 4, Y2 Spring Test 5, Y2 Spring Test 6
5	$8 \times 5 = \square$	40	1	2C6	Y2 Spring Test 1, Y2 Spring Test 2
6	$2 + 9 + 8 = \square$	19	1	2C2a, 2C2b	Y2 Autumn Test 4
7	$19 - 7 = \square$	12	1	2C1	Y1 Summer Test 3, Y1 Summer Test 4
8	$45 - 20 = \square$	25	1	2C2a, 2C2b	Y2 Autumn Test 5
9	$35 - 6 = \square$	29	1	2C2a, 2C2b	Y2 Autumn Test 2
10	$403 + 7 = \square$	410	1	3C1	Y3 Autumn Test 2
11	$\square = 438 + 50$	488	1	3C1	Y3 Autumn Test 3
12	$\frac{1}{4}$ of $20 = \square$	5	1	2F1a	Y2 Summer Test 3
13	$24 + 46 = \square$	70	1	2C2a, 2C2b	Y2 Summer Test 1
14	$3 \times 11 = \square$	33	1	3C6	Y3 Spring Test 3
15	$234 + 100 = \square$	334	1	3N2b	Y3 Autumn Test 3
16	$60 \div \square = 12$	5	1	3C8	Y3 Spring Test 4, Y3 Summer Test 6
17	$643 - 400 = \square$	243	1	3C1	Y3 Autumn Test 3
18	$\frac{6}{10} - \frac{4}{10} = \square$	$\frac{2}{10}$	1	3F1a	Y3 Autumn Test 5, Y3 Spring Test 1
19	$\square = \frac{1}{4} + \frac{2}{4}$	$\frac{3}{4}$	1	3F4	Y3 Autumn Test 5, Y3 Autumn Test 6, Y3 Summer Test 2
20	$8 \times 7 = \square$	56	1	3C6	Y3 Spring Test 5
21	$\square = \frac{3}{5}$ of 10	6	1	3F1b	Y3 Autumn Test 6, Y3 Summer Test 2, Y3 Summer Test 3
22	$375 + 378 = \square$	753	1	3C2	Y3 Autumn Test 4
23	$52 \times 3 = \square$	156	1	3C7	Y3 Spring Test 6, Y3 Summer Test 5
24	$477 - 287 = \square$	190	1	3C2	Y3 Summer Test 1
25	$463 + \square = 721$	258	1	3C4	Y3 Autumn Test 4, Y3 Summer Test 6

Autumn Test 4

1 $7 - 6 = $ ☐

2 $9 - $ ☐ $= 9$

3 $40 - 10 - 10 = $ ☐

4 $8 \div 2 = $ ☐

5 $8 \times 5 = $ ☐

6 $2 + 9 + 8 = $ ☐

7 $19 - 7 = $ ☐

8 $45 - 20 = $ ☐

9 $35 - 6 = $ ☐

10 $403 + 7 = $ ☐

11 ☐ $= 438 + 50$

12 $\frac{1}{4}$ of $20 = $ ☐

13 $24 + 46 = $ ☐

14 $3 \times 11 = $ ☐

Autumn Test 4 (continued)

15 $234 + 100 = \boxed{}$ □

16 $60 \div \boxed{} = 12$ □

17 $643 - 400 = \boxed{}$ □

18 $\dfrac{6}{10} - \dfrac{4}{10} = \boxed{}$ □

19 $\boxed{} = \dfrac{1}{4} + \dfrac{2}{4}$ □

20 $8 \times 7 = \boxed{}$ □

21 $\boxed{} = \dfrac{3}{5}$ of 10 □

22 $375 + 378 = \boxed{}$ □

23 $52 \times 3 = \boxed{}$ □

24 $477 - 287 = \boxed{}$ □

25 $463 + \boxed{} = 721$ □

Total marks	/25

How well did you do?
Colour the numbers of the questions you got correct.

+	6	10	13	15	19	22	25	
−	1	2	3	7	8	9	17	18	24
×	5	14	20	23				
÷	4			16				
Fractions	11	12	18	19	21			
Missing numbers	2	16	25					

Arithmetic Practice Tests Set B Year 3 © Rising Stars UK Ltd 2017

Autumn Test 5

Teacher guidance

25 minutes

Skills and knowledge covered in this test:

- Count from 0 in multiples of 4, 8, 50 and 100 [3N1b]
- Find 10 or 100 more or less than a given number [3N2b]
- Add and subtract mentally [3C1]
- Add and subtract using formal written methods of columnar addition and subtraction [3C2]
- Solve addition and subtraction problems including missing numbers [3C4]
- Recall multiplication and division facts for the 3, 4 and 8 multiplication tables [3C6]

- Calculate multiplication and division statements mentally and using formal written methods [3C7]
- Solve multiplication and division problems including missing numbers [3C8]
- Count up and down in tenths [3F1a]
- Find fractions of a discrete set of objects [3F1b]
- Add and subtract fractions with the same denominator [3F4]

Focus activity: Add and subtract fractions with the same denominator within one whole

3F4

You will need: strips of paper of identical length.

 Step 1 Prepare some strips of paper with a length relevant to the fraction to be explored. For easily folded fractions such as $\frac{1}{8}$, $\frac{1}{4}$ and $\frac{1}{2}$, use any reasonable length. For other fractions, ensure that the whole and fraction parts can all be measured in whole centimetres. For example, use a 20 cm strip for fifths, with each $\frac{1}{5}$ measuring 4 cm.

 Step 2 Give children two identical strips of paper. Ask them to label the first strip 1. Fold or measure then cut the second strip into the appropriate fractions, labelling each fraction piece.

 Step 3 Ask children to take one fraction piece and record how much they have, e.g. $\frac{1}{5}$. Ask children to take a second piece and record how much they have now, e.g. $\frac{2}{5}$. Continue to $\frac{5}{5}$ and ask children to compare this with the strip labelled 1. Confirm that they are equivalent: $\frac{5}{5} = 1$.

 Step 4 Use the fraction pieces to explore addition and subtraction, recording the matching number statement, e.g. 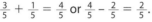 $\frac{3}{5} + \frac{1}{5} = \frac{4}{5}$ or $\frac{4}{5} - \frac{2}{5} = \frac{2}{5}$.

 Step 5 Use the same method to explore adding and subtracting other fractions with the same denominator, taking care to explore only one denominator during any session.

Qu. No.	Question	Answer	Mark	Domain ref.	Focus activity
1	$8 - 8 = \square$	0	1	1C1	Y1 Autumn Test 4, Y1 Spring Test 1
2	$3 \times 2 = \square$	6	1	2C6	Y2 Spring Test 1, Y2 Spring Test 2
3	$7 - \square = 6$	1	1	1C4	Y1 Spring Test 5, Y1 Summer Test 6
4	$11 - 8 = \square$	3	1	2C1	Y1 Summer Test 3, Y1 Summer Test 4
5	$31 + 40 = \square$	71	1	2C2a, 2C2b	Y2 Autumn Test 5
6	$\square = 50 \div 10$	5	1	2C6	Y2 Spring Test 3, Y2 Spring Test 4, Y2 Spring Test 5, Y2 Spring Test 6
7	$70 + 10 + 10 = \square$	90	1	2N1	Y2 Autumn Test 5
8	$62 + 7 = \square$	69	1	2C2a, 2C2b	Y2 Autumn Test 1
9	$\frac{1}{2}$ of $4 = \square$	2	1	2F1a	Y2 Summer Test 3
10	$639 - 3 = \square$	636	1	3C1	Y3 Autumn Test 2
11	$53 - 25 = \square$	28	1	2C2a, 2C2b	Y2 Summer Test 2
12	$175 - 10 = \square$	165	1	3N2b	Y3 Autumn Test 3
13	$6 + 9 + 5 = \square$	20	1	2C2a, 2C2b	Y2 Autumn Test 4
14	$8 \times 4 = \square$	32	1	3C6	Y3 Spring Test 5
15	$\frac{3}{10} - \frac{1}{10} = \square$	$\frac{2}{10}$	1	3F1a	Y3 Autumn Test 5, Y3 Spring Test 1
16	$\frac{3}{4}$ of $4 = \square$	3	1	2F1a	Y2 Summer Test 3
17	$3 \times 9 = \square$	27	1	3C6	Y3 Spring Test 3, Y3 Spring Test 5
18	$\frac{1}{8}$ of $16 = \square$	2	1	3F1b	Y3 Summer Test 3
19	$265 + 495 = \square$	760	1	3C2	Y3 Autumn Test 4
20	$564 - 100 = \square$	464	1	3N2b	Y3 Autumn Test 3
21	$\frac{2}{6} + \frac{3}{6} = \square$	$\frac{5}{6}$	1	3F4	Y3 Autumn Test 5
22	$\square = 48 \times 2$	96	1	3C7	Y3 Spring Test 6, Y3 Summer Test 5
23	$\square + 435 = 643$	208	1	3C4	Y3 Autumn Test 4, Y3 Summer Test 6
24	$\frac{5}{8} - \frac{2}{8} = \square$	$\frac{3}{8}$	1	3F4	Y3 Autumn Test 5
25	$\square \div 3 = 13$	39	1	3C8	Y3 Spring Test 4, Y3 Summer Test 6

Autumn Test 5

Name: .... **Class:** .... **Date:** ....

1 $8 - 8 = \boxed{}$

2 $3 \times 2 = \boxed{}$

3 $7 - \boxed{} = 6$

4 $11 - 8 = \boxed{}$

5 $31 + 40 = \boxed{}$

6 $\boxed{} = 50 \div 10$

7 $70 + 10 + 10 = \boxed{}$

8 $62 + 7 = \boxed{}$

9 $\frac{1}{2}$ of $4 = \boxed{}$

10 $639 - 3 = \boxed{}$

11 $53 - 25 = \boxed{}$

12 $175 - 10 = \boxed{}$

13 $6 + 9 + 5 = \boxed{}$

14 $8 \times 4 = \boxed{}$

Autumn Test 5 (continued)

15 $\dfrac{3}{10} - \dfrac{1}{10} = \boxed{}$ ☐

16 $\dfrac{3}{4}$ of $4 = \boxed{}$ ☐

17 $3 \times 9 = \boxed{}$ ☐

18 $\dfrac{1}{8}$ of $16 = \boxed{}$ ☐

19 $265 + 495 = \boxed{}$ ☐

20 $564 - 100 = \boxed{}$ ☐

21 $\dfrac{2}{6} + \dfrac{3}{6} = \boxed{}$ ☐

22 $\boxed{} = 48 \times 2$ ☐

23 $\boxed{} + 435 = 643$ ☐

24 $\dfrac{5}{8} - \dfrac{2}{8} = \boxed{}$ ☐

25 $\boxed{} \div 3 = 13$ ☐

Total marks	/25

+	5	7	8	13	15	19	21			
−	1	3	4	10	11	12	15	20	23	24
×	2	14	17	22						
÷	6	25								
Fractions	9	15	16	18	21	24				
Missing numbers	3	23	25							

How well did you do?
Colour the numbers of the questions you got correct.

Autumn Test 6

Teacher guidance

(25 minutes)

Skills and knowledge covered in this test:

- Count from 0 in multiples of 4, 8, 50 and 100 [3N1b]
- Find 10 or 100 more or less than a given number [3N2b]
- Add and subtract mentally [3C1]
- Add and subtract using formal written methods of columnar addition and subtraction [3C2]
- Solve addition and subtraction problems including missing numbers [3C4]
- Recall multiplication and division facts for the 3, 4 and 8 multiplication tables [3C6]
- Calculate multiplication and division statements mentally and using formal written methods [3C7]
- Solve multiplication and division problems including missing numbers [3C8]
- Count up and down in tenths [3F1a]
- Find fractions of a discrete set of objects [3F1b]
- Add and subtract fractions with the same denominator [3F4]

Focus activity: Non-unit fractions

3F1b

You will need: strips of paper, scissors, counting objects, 2-D shapes.

 Step 1 Choose a non-unit fraction such as $\frac{2}{3}$. Give children each a strip of paper to explore folding and cutting to make thirds, e.g. they fold a strip of paper into three equal parts, label each part $\frac{1}{3}$ and then shade in two of the thirds to represent $\frac{2}{3}$.

 Step 2 Display the written format of the fraction and discuss the name and meaning of each part.

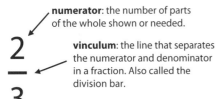

numerator: the number of parts of the whole shown or needed.

vinculum: the line that separates the numerator and denominator in a fraction. Also called the division bar.

denominator: the number of parts the whole has been divided into. Also called the divisor.

$$\frac{2}{3}$$

 Step 3 Ask children to use 2-D shapes or collections of objects to show further examples of the chosen fraction, e.g. give children nine counters and ask them to find one third of the counters and then two thirds of the counters.

 Step 4 Repeat with a different fraction, asking children to explain what they are doing at each step and to use the correct language when they describe its written format.

Qu. No.	Question	Answer	Mark	Domain ref.	Focus activity
1	$2 + 5 = \square$	7	1	1C1	Y1 Autumn Test 2, Y1 Summer Test 4
2	$5 - \square = 3$	2	1	1C4	Y1 Spring Test 1, Y1 Spring Test 5, Y1 Summer Test 4, Y1 Summer Test 6
3	$9 \times 10 = \square$	90	1	2C6	Y2 Spring Test 1, Y2 Spring Test 2
4	$18 - 8 = \square$	10	1	2C1	Y1 Summer Test 3, Y1 Summer Test 4
5	$745 + 100 = \square$	845	1	3N2b	Y3 Autumn Test 3
6	$\frac{1}{3}$ of $3 = \square$	1	1	2F1a	Y2 Summer Test 3
7	$\square = 67 + 30$	97	1	2C2a, 2C2b	Y2 Autumn Test 5
8	$90 - 10 - 10 = \square$	70	1	2N1	Y2 Autumn Test 5
9	$50 - 4 = \square$	46	1	2C2a, 2C2b	Y2 Autumn Test 2
10	$16 \div 2 = \square$	8	1	2C6	Y2 Spring Test 3, Y2 Spring Test 4, Y2 Spring Test 5, Y2 Spring Test 6
11	$319 + 5 = \square$	324	1	3C1	Y3 Autumn Test 2
12	$82 - 48 = \square$	34	1	2C2a, 2C2b	Y2 Summer Test 2
13	$6 + 3 + 8 = \square$	17	1	2C2a, 2C2b	Y2 Autumn Test 4
14	$\frac{1}{4}$ of $12 = \square$	3	1	2F1a	Y2 Summer Test 3
15	$512 + 354 = \square$	866	1	3C2	Y3 Autumn Test 4
16	$\square = 4 \times 8$	32	1	3C6	Y3 Spring Test 3, Y3 Spring Test 5
17	$938 - 500 = \square$	438	1	3C1	Y3 Autumn Test 3
18	$5 \times \square = 45$	9	1	3C8	Y3 Spring Test 4, Y3 Summer Test 6
19	$350 - 167 = \square$	183	1	3C2	Y3 Summer Test 1
20	$\frac{1}{10} + \frac{6}{10} = \square$	$\frac{7}{10}$	1	3F1a	Y3 Autumn Test 5, Y3 Spring Test 1
21	$546 - \square = 243$	303	1	3C4	Y3 Summer Test 6
22	$8 \times 9 = \square$	72	1	3C6	Y3 Spring Test 5
23	$\frac{3}{7} - \frac{1}{7} = \square$	$\frac{2}{7}$	1	3F4	Y3 Autumn Test 5
24	$34 \times 8 = \square$	272	1	3C7	Y3 Spring Test 6, Y3 Summer Test 5
25	$\frac{2}{5}$ of $20 = \square$	8	1	3F1b	Y3 Autumn Test 6, Y3 Summer Test 3

Autumn Test 6

1 $2 + 5 = \boxed{}$

2 $5 - \boxed{} = 3$

3 $9 \times 10 = \boxed{}$

4 $18 - 8 = \boxed{}$

5 $745 + 100 = \boxed{}$

6 $\frac{1}{3}$ of $3 = \boxed{}$

7 $\boxed{} = 67 + 30$

8 $90 - 10 - 10 = \boxed{}$

9 $50 - 4 = \boxed{}$

10 $16 \div 2 = \boxed{}$

11 $319 + 5 = \boxed{}$

12 $82 - 48 = \boxed{}$

13 $6 + 3 + 8 = \boxed{}$

14 $\frac{1}{4}$ of $12 = \boxed{}$

Autumn Test 6 (continued)

15 $512 + 354 = \boxed{}$

16 $\boxed{} = 4 \times 8$

17 $938 - 500 = \boxed{}$

18 $5 \times \boxed{} = 45$

19 $350 - 167 = \boxed{}$

20 $\frac{1}{10} + \frac{6}{10} = \boxed{}$

21 $546 - \boxed{} = 243$

22 $8 \times 9 = \boxed{}$

23 $\frac{3}{7} - \frac{1}{7} = \boxed{}$

24 $34 \times 8 = \boxed{}$

25 $\frac{2}{5}$ of $20 = \boxed{}$

Total marks | **/25**

How well did you do?
Colour the numbers of the
questions you got correct.

+	1	5	7	11	13	15	20		
−	2	4	8	9	12	17	19	21	23
×	3	16	18	22	24				
÷		10							
Fractions	6	14	20	23	25				
Missing numbers	2	18	21						

Arithmetic Practice Tests Set B Year 3 © Rising Stars UK Ltd 2017

Spring Test 1
Teacher guidance

25 minutes

Skills and knowledge covered in this test:

- Count from 0 in multiples of 4, 8, 50 and 100 [3N1b]
- Find 10 or 100 more or less than a given number [3N2b]
- Add and subtract mentally [3C1]
- Add and subtract using formal written methods of columnar addition and subtraction [3C2]
- Solve addition and subtraction problems including missing numbers [3C4]
- Recall multiplication and division facts for the 3, 4 and 8 multiplication tables [3C6]
- Calculate multiplication and division statements mentally and using formal written methods [3C7]
- Solve multiplication and division problems including missing numbers [3C8]
- Count up and down in tenths [3F1a]
- Find fractions of a discrete set of objects [3F1b]
- Add and subtract fractions with the same denominator [3F4]

Focus activity: Adding and subtracting tenths

3F1a, 3F4

You will need: strips of plain paper 20 cm long, or strips of 2 cm squared paper 10 squares long, a dice, scissors.

Step 1 Label the first strip as 1. Fold or measure and cut the second strip to make tenths.

Step 2 Children play the game in pairs. Player 1 has a whole strip and a pile of ten tenths. Player 2 has a whole strip and ten tenths lined up to match the whole.

Step 3 Player 1 is aiming to make 1 from their ten tenths and Player 2 is aiming to reach zero, having removed all their ten tenths.

Step 4 Players take it in turns to roll the dice and line up (Player 1) or remove (Player 2) that number of tenths to reach their goal. The dice shows them how many tenths to move. Players score one point for reaching their goal first. The first player to reach ten points is the winner.

Step 5 Play the game one last time, recording each turn. So if Player 1 rolled a 2 then a 3, they would record $0 + \frac{2}{10} = \frac{2}{10}$; $\frac{2}{10} + \frac{3}{10} = \frac{5}{10}$. If Player 2 rolled a 4 then a 1, they would record this as $\frac{10}{10} - \frac{4}{10} = \frac{6}{10}$; $\frac{6}{10} - \frac{1}{10} = \frac{5}{10}$. Continue play to find the winner, recording each turn.

Qu. No.	Question	Answer	Mark	Domain ref.	Focus activity
1	$7 + 0 = \square$	7	1	1C1	Y1 Autumn Test 2, Y1 Summer Test 4
2	$7 - \square = 2$	5	1	1C4	Y1 Spring Test 1, Y1 Spring Test 5, Y1 Summer Test 4, Y1 Summer Test 6
3	$\frac{1}{2}$ of $24 = \square$	12	1	2F1a	Y2 Summer Test 3
4	$16 - 4 = \square$	12	1	2C1	Y1 Summer Test 3, Y1 Summer Test 4
5	$6 \times 5 = \square$	30	1	2C6	Y2 Spring Test 1, Y2 Spring Test 2
6	$\square = 9 + 8 + 1$	18	1	2C2a, 2C2b	Y2 Autumn Test 4
7	$60 - 10 - 10 = \square$	40	1	2N1	Y2 Autumn Test 5
8	$36 + 8 = \square$	44	1	2C2a, 2C2b	Y2 Autumn Test 1
9	$645 - \square = 100$	545	1	3N2b	Y3 Summer Test 1, Y3 Summer Test 6
10	$93 - 40 = \square$	53	1	2C2a, 2C2b	Y2 Autumn Test 5
11	$3 \times 7 = \square$	21	1	3C6	Y3 Spring Test 3, Y3 Spring Test 5
12	$\frac{2}{10} + \frac{6}{10} = \square$	$\frac{8}{10}$	1	3F1a	Y3 Spring Test 1
13	$30 \div 10 = \square$	3	1	3C6	Y2 Spring Test 3, Y2 Spring Test 4, Y2 Spring Test 5, Y2 Spring Test 6
14	$732 - 30 = \square$	702	1	3C1	Y3 Autumn Test 3
15	$\square = \frac{1}{3}$ of 21	7	1	2F1a	Y2 Summer Test 3
16	$793 + 8 = \square$	801	1	3C1	Y3 Autumn Test 2
17	$548 + 295 = \square$	843	1	3C2	Y3 Autumn Test 4
18	$8 \times 6 = \square$	48	1	3C6	Y3 Spring Test 5
19	$\square \times 3 = 27$	9	1	3C8	Y3 Spring Test 3, Y3 Spring Test 4, Y3 Summer Test 6
20	$613 - 355 = \square$	258	1	3C2	Y3 Summer Test 1
21	$\frac{7}{10} - \frac{4}{10} = \square$	$\frac{3}{10}$	1	3F1a	Y3 Autumn Test 5, Y3 Spring Test 1
22	$\square - 256 = 650$	906	1	3C4	Y3 Summer Test 1, Y3 Summer Test 6
23	$\frac{2}{3}$ of $9 = \square$	6	1	3F1b	Y3 Autumn Test 6, Y3 Summer Test 3
24	$\frac{2}{5} + \frac{1}{5} = \square$	$\frac{3}{5}$	1	3F4	Y3 Autumn Test 5
25	$\square = 48 \times 3$	144	1	3C7	Y3 Spring Test 6, Y3 Summer Test 5

Spring Test 1

Name: .... **Class:** .... **Date:** ....

1 $7 + 0 = \boxed{}$

2 $7 - \boxed{} = 2$

3 $\frac{1}{2}$ of $24 = \boxed{}$

4 $16 - 4 = \boxed{}$

5 $6 \times 5 = \boxed{}$

6 $\boxed{} = 9 + 8 + 1$

7 $60 - 10 - 10 = \boxed{}$

8 $36 + 8 = \boxed{}$

9 $645 - \boxed{} = 100$

10 $93 - 40 = \boxed{}$

11 $3 \times 7 = \boxed{}$

12 $\frac{2}{10} + \frac{6}{10} = \boxed{}$

13 $30 \div 10 = \boxed{}$

14 $732 - 30 = \boxed{}$

Arithmetic Practice Tests Set B Year 3 © Rising Stars UK Ltd 2017

Spring Test 1 (continued)

15 $\boxed{} = \frac{1}{3}$ of 21 $\quad\square$

16 $793 + 8 = \boxed{}$ $\quad\square$

17 $548 + 295 = \boxed{}$ $\quad\square$

18 $8 \times 6 = \boxed{}$ $\quad\square$

19 $\boxed{} \times 3 = 27$ $\quad\square$

20 $613 - 355 = \boxed{}$ $\quad\square$

21 $\frac{7}{10} - \frac{4}{10} = \boxed{}$ $\quad\square$

22 $\boxed{} - 256 = 650$ $\quad\square$

23 $\frac{2}{3}$ of $9 = \boxed{}$ $\quad\square$

24 $\frac{2}{5} + \frac{1}{5} = \boxed{}$ $\quad\square$

25 $\boxed{} = 48 \times 3$ $\quad\square$

Total marks	/25

How well did you do?
Colour the numbers of the
questions you got correct.

+	1	6	8	12	16	17	24		
−	2	4	7	9	10	14	20	21	22
×	5	11	18	19	25				
÷		13							
Fractions	3	12	13	15	21	23	24		
Missing numbers	2	9	19	22					

Spring Test 2

Teacher guidance

25 minutes

Skills and knowledge covered in this test:

- Count from 0 in multiples of 4, 8, 50 and 100 [3N1b]
- Find 10 or 100 more or less than a given number [3N2b]
- Add and subtract mentally [3C1]
- Add and subtract using formal written methods of columnar addition and subtraction [3C2]
- Solve addition and subtraction problems including missing numbers [3C4]
- Recall multiplication and division facts for the 3, 4 and 8 multiplication tables [3C6]

- Calculate multiplication and division statements mentally and using formal written methods [3C7]
- Solve multiplication and division problems including missing numbers [3C8]
- Count up and down in tenths [3F1a]
- Find fractions of a discrete set of objects [3F1b]
- Add and subtract fractions with the same denominator [3F4]

Focus activity: Partitioning multipliers

3C6, 3C7

You will need: counters.

 Introduce the language of multiplication, multiplicand × multiplier = product and division, dividend ÷ divisor = quotient. Display the vocabulary alongside sample calculations and refer to it frequently.

 Display the following set of calculations:

4×4	$4 \times 2 \times 2$
3×8	$3 \times 4 \times 2$
4×10	$4 \times 5 \times 2$

 Ask children what they notice. On each row, the multiplicand and product stay the same but the multiplier has been partitioned into two parts. It does not matter how we group the quantities when we multiply (or add). This is the associative law. Tell children that it is good to know about the associative law as sometimes we can make calculations easier to do by partitioning them in different ways.

 Challenge children to use counters to create arrays for both calculations on the same row to help them explain what is happening.

 Ask children to say which group of counters is easier to count. Agree that by partitioning the multiplier it is easier to see what the product is by using aaddition to add the two groups of counters.

Qu. No.	Question	Answer	Mark	Domain ref.	Focus activity
1	$9 + 4 = \square$	13	1	1C1	Y1 Summer Test 2, Y1 Summer Test 4
2	$9 - \square = 5$	4	1	1C4	Y1 Spring Test 1, Y1 Spring Test 5, Y1 Summer Test 4, Y1 Summer Test 6
3	$13 - 6 = \square$	7	1	2C1	Y1 Summer Test 3, Y1 Summer Test 4
4	$9 \times 2 = \square$	18	1	2C6	Y2 Spring Test 1, Y2 Spring Test 2
5	$20 + 10 + 10 = \square$	40	1	2N1	Y2 Autumn Test 5
6	$\square = 24 - 7$	17	1	2C2a, 2C2b	Y2 Autumn Test 2
7	$58 - 10 = \square$	48	1	2C2a, 2C2b	Y2 Autumn Test 5
8	$354 + 10 = \square$	364	1	3N2b	Y3 Autumn Test 3
9	$20 \div 5 = \square$	4	1	2C6	Y2 Spring Test 3, Y2 Spring Test 4, Y2 Spring Test 5, Y2 Spring Test 6
10	$802 - 6 = \square$	796	1	3C1	Y3 Autumn Test 2
11	$\square = 8 + 8 + 5$	21	1	2C2a, 2C2b	Y2 Autumn Test 4
12	$68 + 19 = \square$	87	1	2C2a, 2C2b	Y2 Summer Test 1, Y2 Summer Test 6
13	$\frac{1}{4}$ of 40 = $\square$	10	1	2F1a	Y2 Summer Test 3
14	$753 + 200 = \square$	953	1	3C1	Y3 Autumn Test 3
15	$8 \times 5 = \square$	40	1	3C6	Y3 Spring Test 5
16	$\square = 27 \div 3$	9	1	3C6	Y3 Spring Test 3
17	$4 \times 3 = \square$	12	1	3C6	Y3 Spring Test 3, Y3 Spring Test 5
18	$25 \times 5 = \square$	125	1	3C7	Y3 Spring Test 6, Y3 Summer Test 5
19	$344 + 359 = \square$	703	1	3C2	Y3 Autumn Test 4
20	$626 - 375 = \square$	251	1	3C2	Y2 Summer Test 1
21	$\frac{4}{10} + \frac{4}{10} = \square$	$\frac{8}{10}$	1	3F1a	Y3 Autumn Test 5, Y3 Spring Test 1
22	$437 - \square = 278$	159	1	3C4	Y3 Summer Test 1, Y3 Summer Test 6
23	$\square \div 5 = 6$	30	1	3C8	Y3 Spring Test 4, Y3 Summer Test 6
24	$\frac{5}{9} - \frac{1}{9} = \square$	$\frac{4}{9}$	1	3F4	Y3 Autumn Test 5
25	$\frac{3}{8}$ of 40 = $\square$	15	1	3F1b	Y3 Summer Test 3

Spring Test 2

Name: .... Class: .... Date: ....

1 $9 + 4 = \boxed{}$ ☐

2 $9 - \boxed{} = 5$ ☐

3 $13 - 6 = \boxed{}$ ☐

4 $9 \times 2 = \boxed{}$ ☐

5 $20 + 10 + 10 = \boxed{}$ ☐

6 $\boxed{} = 24 - 7$ ☐

7 $58 - 10 = \boxed{}$ ☐

8 $354 + 10 = \boxed{}$ ☐

9 $20 \div 5 = \boxed{}$ ☐

10 $802 - 6 = \boxed{}$ ☐

11 $\boxed{} = 8 + 8 + 5$ ☐

12 $68 + 19 = \boxed{}$ ☐

13 $\frac{1}{4}$ of $40 = \boxed{}$ ☐

14 $753 + 200 = \boxed{}$ ☐

Spring Test 2 (continued)

15 $8 \times 5 = $ ☐

16 ☐ $= 27 \div 3$

17 $4 \times 3 = $ ☐

18 $25 \times 5 = $ ☐

19 $344 + 359 = $ ☐

20 $626 - 375 = $ ☐

21 $\frac{4}{10} + \frac{4}{10} = $ ☐

22 $437 - $ ☐ $= 278$

23 ☐ $\div 5 = 6$

24 $\frac{5}{9} - \frac{1}{9} = $ ☐

25 $\frac{3}{8}$ of $40 = $ ☐

Total marks	**/25**

How well did you do?
Colour the numbers of the questions you got correct.

+	1	5	8	11	12	14	19	21
−	2	3	6	7	10	20	22	24
×	4	15	17	18	23	25		
÷	9		23					
Fractions	13	16	21	24	25			
Missing numbers	2	22	23					

Arithmetic Practice Tests Set B Year 3 © Rising Stars UK Ltd 2017

Spring Test 3
Teacher guidance

25 minutes

Skills and knowledge covered in this test:

- Count from 0 in multiples of 4, 8, 50 and 100 [3N1b]
- Find 10 or 100 more or less than a given number [3N2b]
- Add and subtract mentally [3C1]
- Add and subtract using formal written methods of columnar addition and subtraction [3C2]
- Solve addition and subtraction problems including missing numbers [3C4]
- Recall multiplication and division facts for the 3, 4 and 8 multiplication tables [3C6]

- Calculate multiplication and division statements mentally and using formal written methods [3C7]
- Solve multiplication and division problems including missing numbers [3C8]
- Count up and down in tenths [3F1a]
- Find fractions of a discrete set of objects [3F1b]
- Add and subtract fractions with the same denominator [3F4]

Focus activity: Multiplication table for 3

3C6

You will need: identical objects or images with an inherent threeness, e.g. triangles, sticks of three cubes, pictures of tricycles.

 Build and record the multiplication table for 3. Use an object with an inherent threeness to illustrate the increasing number of threes in the multiplication table.

$3 \times 0 = 0$

$3 \times 1 = 3$

$3 \times 2 = 6$

$3 \times 3 = 9$

$3 \times 4 = 12$

and so on.

 Practise reading and exploring the patterns in the multiplication table by reading the multiplication facts and relating them to the number of threes in the objects next to each fact. Link facts such as 3×2 and 3×4, showing how, as the multiplier doubles, so does the number of triangles.

 Play $\times 3$ bingo. Children fold a piece of A5 paper into four and write a different product from the multiplication table for 3 in each space.

 Call out a multiplication fact, without the product, for children to calculate and cross off their bingo card if they have it. Use more complex descriptions of the multiplication fact, for example half of 3×4 (3×2) or double 3×5 (3×10).

 Challenge the winner to call out the clues for a second game.

Qu. No.	Question	Answer	Mark	Domain ref.	Focus activity
1	$4 - 3 = \square$	1	1	1C1	Y1 Autumn Test 4, Y1 Summer Test 4
2	$8 - \square = 6$	2	1	1C4	Y1 Spring Test 1, Y1 Spring Test 5, Y1 Summer Test 4, Y1 Summer Test 6
3	$\square = \frac{3}{4}$ of 20	15	1	2F1a	Y2 Summer Test 3
4	$7 \times 10 = \square$	70	1	2C6	Y2 Spring Test 1, Y2 Spring Test 2
5	$15 - 9 = \square$	6	1	2C1	Y1 Summer Test 3, Y1 Summer Test 4
6	$4 + 7 + 6 = \square$	17	1	2C2a, 2C2b	Y2 Autumn Test 4
7	$65 - 8 = \square$	57	1	2C2a, 2C2b	Y2 Autumn Test 2
8	$100 - 10 - 10 = \square$	80	1	2N1	Y2 Autumn Test 5
9	$25 \div 5 = \square$	5	1	2C6	Y2 Spring Test 3, Y2 Spring Test 4, Y2 Spring Test 5, Y2 Spring Test 6
10	$29 + 50 = \square$	79	1	2C2a, 2C2b	Y2 Autumn Test 5
11	$224 + 50 + 50 = \square$	324	1	3N1b	Y3 Autumn Test 3
12	$75 - 38 = \square$	37	1	2C2a, 2C2b	Y2 Summer Test 2
13	$152 + 6 = \square$	158	1	3C1	Y3 Autumn Test 2
14	$3 \times 3 = \square$	9	1	3C6	Y3 Spring Test 3, Y3 Spring Test 5
15	$\square = 426 - 10$	416	1	3N2b	Y3 Autumn Test 3
16	$283 + 40 = \square$	323	1	3C1	Y3 Autumn Test 3
17	$8 \times 8 = \square$	64	1	3C6	Y3 Spring Test 5
18	$385 + 594 = \square$	979	1	3C2	Y3 Autumn Test 4
19	$41 \times 3 = \square$	123	1	3C7	Y3 Spring Test 6, Y3 Summer Test 5
20	$942 - 437 = \square$	505	1	3C2	Y2 Summer Test 1
21	$\square \times 4 = 32$	8	1	3C8	Y3 Spring Test 4, Y3 Summer Test 6
22	$\square + 634 = 812$	178	1	3C4	Y3 Autumn Test 4, Y3 Summer Test 6
23	$\frac{2}{10} + \frac{5}{10} = \square$	$\frac{7}{10}$	1	3F1a	Y3 Autumn Test 5, Y3 Spring Test 1
24	$\square = \frac{6}{7} - \frac{4}{7}$	$\frac{2}{7}$	1	3F4	Y3 Autumn Test 5
25	$\frac{2}{3}$ of 15 = $\square$	10	1	3F1b	Y3 Summer Test 3

Spring Test 3

1 $4 - 3 = \boxed{}$

2 $8 - \boxed{} = 6$

3 $\boxed{} = \frac{3}{4}$ of 20

4 $7 \times 10 = \boxed{}$

5 $15 - 9 = \boxed{}$

6 $4 + 7 + 6 = \boxed{}$

7 $65 - 8 = \boxed{}$

8 $100 - 10 - 10 = \boxed{}$

9 $25 \div 5 = \boxed{}$

10 $29 + 50 = \boxed{}$

11 $224 + 50 + 50 = \boxed{}$

12 $75 - 38 = \boxed{}$

13 $152 + 6 = \boxed{}$

14 $3 \times 3 = \boxed{}$

Arithmetic Practice Tests Set B Year 3 © Rising Stars UK Ltd 2017

Spring Test 3 (continued)

15 ☐ $= 426 - 10$

16 $283 + 40 =$ ☐

17 $8 \times 8 =$ ☐

18 $385 + 594 =$ ☐

19 $41 \times 3 =$ ☐

20 $942 - 437 =$ ☐

21 ☐ $\times 4 = 32$

22 ☐ $+ 634 = 812$

23 $\frac{2}{10} + \frac{5}{10} =$ ☐

24 ☐ $= \frac{6}{7} - \frac{4}{7}$

25 $\frac{2}{3}$ of $15 =$ ☐

Total marks	/25

How well did you do?
Colour the numbers of the questions you got correct.

+	6	10	11	13	16	18	22	23		
−	1	2		5	7	8	12	20		24
×	4	14	17	19	21					
÷	9	15	21							
Fractions	3	15	23	24	25					
Missing numbers	2	21	22							

Spring Test 4

Teacher guidance

25 minutes

Skills and knowledge covered in this test:

- Count from 0 in multiples of 4, 8, 50 and 100 [3N1b]
- Find 10 or 100 more or less than a given number [3N2b]
- Add and subtract mentally [3C1]
- Add and subtract using formal written methods of columnar addition and subtraction [3C2]
- Solve addition and subtraction problems including missing numbers [3C4]
- Recall multiplication and division facts for the 3, 4 and 8 multiplication tables [3C6]

- Calculate multiplication and division statements mentally and using formal written methods [3C7]
- Solve multiplication and division problems including missing numbers [3C8]
- Count up and down in tenths [3F1a]
- Find fractions of a discrete set of objects [3F1b]
- Add and subtract fractions with the same denominator [3F4]

Focus activity: Fact families and missing numbers

3C6, 3C7, 3C8

You will need: small counting objects.

 Choose a known multiplication fact such as $5 \times 3 = 15$. Ask children to make an array, using counters or cubes, to show this fact.

 Confirm that the 5 and the 3 can be multiplied together in any order, so the multiplication calculation for the array can be written as $5 \times 3 = 15$ or $3 \times 5 = 15$. Beginning with the whole, the product, the statements are $15 = 5 \times 3$, $15 = 3 \times 5$.

 Ask children to look again at the array and write two matching division statements: $15 \div 5 = 3$ and $15 \div 3 = 5$. Beginning with the quotient, the statements are $3 = 15 \div 5$ and $5 = 15 \div 3$.

 List all eight facts in the fact family and display this clearly for children to see.

 Give children plenty of practice at listing fact families so they can link the facts and use them to find missing numbers, e.g.

$\square \times 3 = 15 \rightarrow 3 \times \square = 15$ or $15 = 3 \times \square$

$\square \div 5 = 6 \rightarrow 6 = \square \div 5$ or $6 \times 5 = \square$

$22 \div \square = 2 \rightarrow 22 \div 2 = \square$

Qu. No.	Question	Answer	Mark	Domain ref.	Focus activity
1	$5 + 5 = \square$	10	1	1C1	Y1 Autumn Test 6, Y 1 Summer Test 4
2	$4 - \square = 4$	0	1	1C4	Y1 Spring Test 1, Y1 Spring Test 5, Y1 Summer Test 4, Y1 Summer Test 6
3	$\square = 4 \times 10$	40	1	2C6	Y2 Spring Test 1, Y2 Spring Test 2
4	$14 - 3 = \square$	11	1	2C1	Y1 Summer Test 3, Y1 Summer Test 4
5	$30 - 10 - 10 = \square$	10	1	2N1	Y2 Autumn Test 5
6	$745 - 100 = \square$	645	1	3N2b	Y3 Autumn Test 3
7	$25 + 56 = \square$	81	1	2C2a, 2C2b	Y2 Summer Test 1
8	$22 \div \square = 2$	11	1	2C6	Y2 Spring Test 5, Y2 Spring Test 6, Y2 Summer Test 5
9	$83 - 70 = \square$	13	1	2C2a, 2C2b	Y2 Autumn Test 5
10	$9 + 4 + 7 = \square$	20	1	2C2a, 2C2b	Y2 Autumn Test 4
11	$\frac{1}{4}$ of $16 = \square$	4	1	2F1a	Y2 Summer Test 3
12	$\frac{1}{3}$ of $30 = \square$	10	1	2F1a	Y2 Summer Test 3
13	$\square = 56 \div 8$	7	1	3C6	Y3 Spring Test 5
14	$634 - 8 = \square$	626	1	3C1	Y3 Autumn Test 2
15	$798 - 80 = \square$	718	1	3C1	Y3 Autumn Test 3
16	$421 + 288 = \square$	709	1	3C2	Y3 Autumn Test 4
17	$8 \times 4 = \square$	32	1	3C6	Y3 Spring Test 5
18	$3 \times 6 = \square$	18	1	3C6	Y3 Spring Test 3, Y3 Spring Test 5
19	$354 + 595 = \square$	949	1	3C2	Y3 Autumn Test 4
20	$\frac{9}{10} - \frac{8}{10} = \square$	$\frac{1}{10}$	1	3F1b	Y3 Autumn Test 5, Y3 Summer Test 3
21	$28 \div \square = 7$	4	1	3C8	Y3 Spring Test 4, Y3 Summer Test 6
22	$532 + \square = 904$	372	1	3C4	Y3 Autumn Test 4, Y3 Summer Test 6
23	$24 \times 8 = \square$	192	1	3C7	Y3 Spring Test 6, Y3 Summer Test 5
24	$\square = \frac{2}{5} + \frac{2}{5}$	$\frac{4}{5}$	1	3F4	Y3 Autumn Test 5
25	$\frac{4}{5}$ of $10 = \square$	8	1	3F1b	Y3 Summer Test 3

Spring Test 4

Name: .... Class: .... Date: ....

1 $5 + 5 = \boxed{}$

2 $4 - \boxed{} = 4$

3 $\boxed{} = 4 \times 10$

4 $14 - 3 = \boxed{}$

5 $30 - 10 - 10 = \boxed{}$

6 $745 - 100 = \boxed{}$

7 $25 + 56 = \boxed{}$

8 $22 \div \boxed{} = 2$

9 $83 - 70 = \boxed{}$

10 $9 + 4 + 7 = \boxed{}$

11 $\frac{1}{4}$ of $16 = \boxed{}$

12 $\frac{1}{3}$ of $30 = \boxed{}$

13 $\boxed{} = 56 \div 8$

14 $634 - 8 = \boxed{}$

Spring Test 4 (continued)

15 $798 - 80 = $ ☐

16 $421 \times 288 = $ ☐

17 $8 \times 4 = $ ☐

18 $3 \times 6 = $ ☐

19 $354 + 595 = $ ☐

20 $\frac{9}{10} - \frac{8}{10} = $ ☐

21 $28 \div \boxed{} = 7$ ☐

22 $532 + \boxed{} = 904$ ☐

23 $24 \times 8 = $ ☐

24 $\boxed{} = \frac{2}{5} + \frac{2}{5}$ ☐

25 $\frac{4}{5}$ of $10 = $ ☐

Total marks	/25

How well did you do?
Colour the numbers of the questions you got correct.

+		1	7	10	15	18	21	23
−		2	4	5	6	9	13	14	19
×		3	16	17	22			
÷		8		13	20			
Fractions		11	12	19	23	24		
Missing numbers		2	8	20	21			

Arithmetic Practice Tests Set B Year 3 © Rising Stars UK Ltd 2017

Spring Test 5

Teacher guidance

25 minutes

Skills and knowledge covered in this test:

- Count from 0 in multiples of 4, 8, 50 and 100 [3N1b]
- Find 10 or 100 more or less than a given number [3N2b]
- Add and subtract mentally [3C1]
- Add and subtract using formal written methods of columnar addition and subtraction [3C2]
- Solve addition and subtraction problems including missing numbers [3C4]
- Recall multiplication and division facts for the 3, 4 and 8 multiplication tables [3C6]

- Calculate multiplication and division statements mentally and using formal written methods [3C7]
- Solve multiplication and division problems including missing numbers [3C8]
- Count up and down in tenths [3F1a]
- Find fractions of a discrete set of objects [3F1b]
- Add and subtract fractions with the same denominator [3F4]

Focus activity: Patterns in multiplication tables for 2, 4 and 8

3C6

 Step 1 Once children have been introduced to the multiplication tables for 2, 4 and 8, draw up a chart of the three tables together as below, continuing to × 12.

$2 \times 0 = 0$	$4 \times 0 = 0$	$8 \times 0 = 0$
$2 \times 1 = 2$	$4 \times 1 = 4$	$8 \times 1 = 8$
$2 \times 2 = 4$	$4 \times 2 = 8$	$8 \times 2 = 16$

 Step 2 Ask children to discuss the patterns they notice. Encourage the correct use of vocabulary so that everyone knows which pattern is being described.

 Step 3 Check that children recognise that the multiplicand and product are both doubled along each row. So the multiplication table for 4 is double that for 2, and the multiplication table for 8 is double that of 4. This also means that the multiplication table for 4 is half of that for 8 and the multiplication table for 2 is half of that for 4.

 Step 4 Draw pairs of arrows to illustrate the patterns noted. Display as a useful reminder.

double
× 2   × 4
halve

double
× 4   × 8
halve

Qu. No.	Question	Answer	Mark	Domain ref.	Focus activity
1	$6 + 3 = \square$	9	1	1C1	Y1 Autumn Test 2, Y1 Summer Test 4
2	$5 - \square = 1$	4	1	1C4	Y1 Spring Test 1, Y1 Spring Test 5, Y1 Summer Test 4, Y1 Summer Test 6
3	$3 \times 5 = \square$	15	1	2C6	Y2 Spring Test 1, Y2 Spring Test 2
4	$8 + 3 + 7 = \square$	18	1	2C2a, 2C2b	Y2 Autumn Test 4
5	$\square = 80 \div 10$	8	1	2C6	Y2 Spring Test 3, Y2 Spring Test 4, Y2 Spring Test 5, Y2 Spring Test 6
6	$17 - 8 = \square$	9	1	2C1	Y1 Summer Test 3, Y1 Summer Test 4
7	$90 - 10 - 10 = \square$	70	1	2N1	Y2 Autumn Test 5
8	$87 - 6 = \square$	81	1	2C2a, 2C2b	Y2 Autumn Test 2
9	$52 + 30 = \square$	82	1	2C2a, 2C2b	Y2 Autumn Test 5
10	$\frac{1}{2}$ of $6 = \square$	3	1	2F1a	Y2 Summer Test 3
11	$633 + 10 = \square$	643	1	3N2b	Y3 Autumn Test 3
12	$264 + 5 = \square$	269	1	3C1	Y3 Autumn Test 2
13	$83 - 35 = \square$	48	1	2C2a, 2C2b	Y2 Summer Test 2
14	$\square = \frac{3}{4}$ of 16	12	1	2F1a	Y2 Summer Test 3
15	$514 - 300 = \square$	214	1	3C1	Y3 Autumn Test 3
16	$4 \times 7 = \square$	28	1	3C6	Y3 Spring Test 3, Y3 Spring Test 5
17	$\square \div 3 = 5$	15	1	3C8	Y3 Spring Test 4, Y3 Summer Test 6
18	$8 \times 6 = \square$	48	1	3C6	Y3 Spring Test 5
19	$354 + 595 = \square$	949	1	3C2	Y3 Autumn Test 4
20	$\frac{5}{10} + \frac{1}{10} = \square$	$\frac{6}{10}$ or $\frac{3}{5}$	1	3F1a	Y3 Autumn Test 5, Y3 Spring Test 1
21	$731 - 355 = \square$	376	1	3C2	Y3 Summer Test 1
22	$\square = \frac{5}{6} - \frac{4}{6}$	$\frac{1}{6}$	1	3F4	Y3 Autumn Test 5
23	$\square - 351 = 648$	999	1	3C4	Y3 Summer Test 1, Y3 Summer Test 6
24	$35 \times 4 = \square$	140	1	3C7	Y3 Spring Test 6, Y3 Summer Test 5
25	$\frac{2}{3}$ of $12 = \square$	8	1	3F1b	Y3 Autumn Test 6, Y3 Summer Test 3

Spring Test 5

1 $6 + 3 =$ ☐

2 $5 - \boxed{} = 1$

3 $3 \times 5 =$ ☐

4 $8 + 3 + 7 =$ ☐

5 $\boxed{} = 80 \div 10$

6 $17 - 8 =$ ☐

7 $90 - 10 - 10 =$ ☐

8 $87 - 6 =$ ☐

9 $52 + 30 =$ ☐

10 $\frac{1}{2}$ of $6 =$ ☐

11 $633 + 10 =$ ☐

12 $264 + 5 =$ ☐

13 $83 - 35 =$ ☐

14 $\boxed{} = \frac{3}{4}$ of 16

Spring Test 5 (continued)

15 $514 - 300 = \boxed{}$

16 $4 \times 7 = \boxed{}$

17 $\boxed{} \div 3 = 5$

18 $8 \times 6 = \boxed{}$

19 $354 + 595 = \boxed{}$

20 $\dfrac{5}{10} + \dfrac{1}{10} = \boxed{}$

21 $731 - 355 = \boxed{}$

22 $\boxed{} = \dfrac{5}{6} - \dfrac{4}{6}$

23 $\boxed{} - 351 = 648$

24 $35 \times 4 = \boxed{}$

25 $\dfrac{2}{3}$ of $12 = \boxed{}$

Total marks	/25

How well did you do?
Colour the numbers of the questions you got correct.

+	1	4	9	11	12	19	20		
−	2	6	7	8	13	15	21	22	23
×	3	16	18	24					
÷	5	17							
Fractions	10	14	20	22	25				
Missing numbers	2	17	23						

Spring Test 6
Teacher guidance

Skills and knowledge covered in this test:

- Count from 0 in multiples of 4, 8, 50 and 100 [3N1b]
- Find 10 or 100 more or less than a given number [3N2b]
- Add and subtract mentally [3C1]
- Add and subtract using formal written methods of columnar addition and subtraction [3C2]
- Solve addition and subtraction problems including missing numbers [3C4]
- Recall multiplication and division facts for the 3, 4 and 8 multiplication tables [3C6]

- Calculate multiplication and division statements mentally and using formal written methods [3C7]
- Solve multiplication and division problems including missing numbers [3C8]
- Count up and down in tenths [3F1a]
- Find fractions of a discrete set of objects [3F1b]
- Add and subtract fractions with the same denominator [3F4]

Focus activity: 2-digit numbers multiplied by a single-digit number

3C7

You will need: Base 10 apparatus, digit cards.

 Make 27 using Base 10 apparatus, laying the tens sticks and ones cubes in one long row. Repeat until there are five rows of 27.

 Add the tens, exchanging ten tens for one hundred. Add the ones, exchanging ten ones for a ten. Lay out the hundreds, tens and ones in order to see the final total of 135: $5 \times 27 = 135$.

 Model a pictorial method by drawing a rectangle to represent an array for the calculation.

 Partition the 27 into 10, 10 and 7 and use this to partition the rectangle appropriately. Children could choose to partition the larger number in other ways.

```
           27
     10    10    7
   ┌─────┬─────┬─────┐
 5 │ 50  │ 50  │ 35  │
   └─────┴─────┴─────┘
```

 Find the product for each part of the rectangle and add them together to find the total: $5 \times 27 = 50 + 50 + 35 = 135$.

 Ask children to shuffle digit cards 1, 2, 3, 4, 5 and 8. They then take the first three cards and use them to create a multiplication calculation $\square \times \square\square =$ to solve using either method. These methods can later be refined to the grid method.

Qu. No.	Question	Answer	Mark	Domain ref.	Focus activity
1	$8 - 5 = \square$	3	1	1C1	Y1 Autumn Test 4, Y1 Summer Test 4
2	$7 \times 2 = \square$	14	1	2C6	Y2 Spring Test 1, Y2 Spring Test 2
3	$12 - 5 = \square$	7	1	2C1	Y1 Summer Test 3, Y1 Summer Test 4
4	$6 - \square = 2$	4	1	1C4	Y1 Spring Test 1, Y1 Spring Test 5, Y1 Summer Test 4, Y1 Summer Test 6
5	$40 + 10 + 10 = \square$	60	1	2N1	Y2 Autumn Test 5
6	$71 + 3 = \square$	74	1	2C2a, 2C2b	Y2 Autumn Test 1
7	$\square = 5 + 8 + 6$	19	1	2C2a, 2C2b	Y2 Autumn Test 4
8	$\frac{1}{3}$ of $18 = \square$	6	1	2F1a	Y2 Summer Test 3
9	$30 \div 5 = \square$	6	1	2C6	Y2 Spring Test 3, Y2 Spring Test 4, Y2 Spring Test 5, Y2 Spring Test 6
10	$33 + 60 = \square$	93	1	2C2a, 2C2b	Y2 Autumn Test 5
11	$852 - 7 = \square$	845	1	3C1	Y3 Autumn Test 2
12	$\square = \frac{1}{4}$ of 24	6	1	2F1a	Y2 Summer Test 3
13	$507 + 50 + 50 = \square$	607	1	3N1b	Y3 Autumn Test 3
14	$52 - 17 = \square$	35	1	2C2a, 2C2b	Y2 Summer Test 2
15	$824 + 100 = \square$	924	1	3N2b	Y3 Autumn Test 3
16	$4 \times 9 = \square$	36	1	3C6	Y3 Spring Test 3, Y3 Spring Test 5
17	$2 \times \square = 18$	9	1	3C8	Y3 Spring Test 4, Y3 Summer Test 6
18	$\square = 432 + 496$	928	1	3C2	Y3 Autumn Test 4
19	$\frac{9}{10} - \frac{3}{10} = \square$	$\frac{6}{10}$	1	3F1a	Y2 Autumn Test 5 , Y3 Spring Test 1
20	$42 \times 4 = \square$	168	1	3C7	Y3 Spring Test 6, Y3 Summer Test 5
21	$803 - 254 = \square$	549	1	3C2	Y3 Summer Test 1
22	$367 + \square = 633$	266	1	3C4	Y3 Autumn Test 4, Y3 Summer Test 6
23	$\frac{1}{5}$ of $5 = \square$	1	1	3F1b	Y3 Summer Test 3
24	$63 \times 6 = \square$	378	1	3C7	Y3 Spring Test 6, Y3 Summer Test 5
25	$\frac{3}{7} + \frac{2}{7} = \square$	$\frac{5}{7}$	1	3F4	Y3 Autumn Test 5

Spring Test 6

Name: .... Class: .... Date: ....

1 $8 - 5 = \boxed{}$

2 $7 \times 2 = \boxed{}$

3 $12 - 5 = \boxed{}$

4 $6 - \boxed{} = 2$

5 $40 + 10 + 10 = \boxed{}$

6 $71 + 3 = \boxed{}$

7 $\boxed{} = 5 + 8 + 6$

8 $\frac{1}{3}$ of $18 = \boxed{}$

9 $30 \div 5 = \boxed{}$

10 $33 + 60 = \boxed{}$

11 $852 - 7 = \boxed{}$

12 $\boxed{} = \frac{1}{4}$ of 24

13 $507 + 50 + 50 = \boxed{}$

14 $52 - 17 = \boxed{}$

Spring Test 6 (continued)

15 $824 + 100 = \boxed{}$

16 $4 \times 9 = \boxed{}$

17 $2 \times \boxed{} = 18$

18 $\boxed{} = 432 + 496$

19 $\frac{9}{10} + \frac{3}{10} = \boxed{}$

20 $42 \times 4 = \boxed{}$

21 $803 - 254 = \boxed{}$

22 $367 + \boxed{} = 633$

23 $\frac{1}{5}$ of $5 = \boxed{}$

24 $63 \times 6 = \boxed{}$

25 $\frac{3}{7} + \frac{2}{7} = \boxed{}$

Total marks	/25

How well did you do?
Colour the numbers of the questions you got correct.

+	5	6	7		10	13	15	18	22	25
−		1	3	4	11	14	19	21		
x		2	16	17	20	24				
÷		9								
Fractions		8	12	19	23	25				
Missing numbers		4	17	22						

Arithmetic Practice Tests Set B Year 3 © Rising Stars UK Ltd 2017

Summer Test 1

Teacher guidance

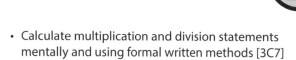

Skills and knowledge covered in this test:

- Count from 0 in multiples of 4, 8, 50 and 100 [3N1b]
- Find 10 or 100 more or less than a given number [3N2b]
- Add and subtract mentally [3C1]
- Add and subtract using formal written methods of columnar addition and subtraction [3C2]
- Solve addition and subtraction problems including missing numbers [3C4]
- Recall multiplication and division facts for the 3, 4 and 8 multiplication tables [3C6]

- Calculate multiplication and division statements mentally and using formal written methods [3C7]
- Solve multiplication and division problems including missing numbers [3C8]
- Count up and down in tenths [3F1a]
- Find fractions of a discrete set of objects [3F1b]
- Add and subtract fractions with the same denominator [3F4]

Focus activity: Developing written methods for subtracting 3-digit numbers

3C2, 3C3

You will need: Base 10 apparatus, place-value cards.

Make a 3-digit number using Base 10 apparatus. Choose a smaller 3-digit number to subtract, but do not make this with apparatus.

Record the calculation in columns.

$$436$$
$$- 148$$

Starting with the ones column and apparatus, subtract 8 from 6. There are insufficient ones cubes to subtract 8, so exchange a ten for ten ones. Record this using the method shown or follow the guidance in your school calculation policy. There are now 16 ones: $16 - 8 = 8$.

$$4\,{}^2 3\,{}^1 6$$
$$-\ 1\ 4\ 8$$
$$\overline{\qquad\ \ 8}$$

Point to the tens column and apparatus and subtract 4 tens from 2 tens. There are not enough tens to subtract 4, so exchange a hundred for ten tens. Record this on the calculation. There are now 12 tens: $12 - 4 = 8$.

$$^3 4\,{}^{12} 3\,{}^1 6$$
$$-\ 1\ 4\ 8$$
$$\overline{\qquad 8\ 8}$$

Point to the hundreds column and apparatus and subtract 1 hundred from 3 hundreds. No exchange is needed: $300 - 100 = 200$.

$$^3 4\,{}^{12} 3\,{}^1 6 \qquad \text{minuend}$$
$$-\ 1\ 4\ 8 \qquad \text{subtrahend}$$
$$\overline{\ \ 2\ 8\ 8} \qquad \text{difference}$$

Check by adding the difference to the subtrahend.

Qu. No.	Question	Answer	Mark	Domain ref.	Focus activity
1	$9 - 6 = \square$	3	1	1C1	Y1 Autumn Test 4, Y1 Summer Test 4
2	$8 - \square = 7$	1	1	1C4	Y1 Spring Test 1, Y1 Spring Test 5, Y1 Summer Test 4, Y1 Summer Test 6
3	$5 \times 11 = \square$	55	1	2C6	Y2 Spring Test 1, Y2 Spring Test 2
4	$16 - 7 = \square$	9	1	2C1	Y1 Summer Test 3, Y1 Summer Test 4
5	$50 - 10 - 10 = \square$	30	1	2N1	Y2 Autumn Test 5
6	$95 - 8 = \square$	87	1	2C2a, 2C2b	Y2 Autumn Test 2
7	$18 \div 2 = \square$	9	1	2C6	Y2 Spring Test 3, Y2 Spring Test 4, Y2 Spring Test 5, Y2 Spring Test 6
8	$48 - 20 = \square$	28	1	2C2a, 2C2b	Y2 Autumn Test 5
9	$6 + 6 + 2 = \square$	14	1	2C2a, 2C2b	Y2 Autumn Test 4
10	$\frac{1}{2}$ of $18 = \square$	9	1	2F1a	Y2 Summer Test 3
11	$\square = 64 + 26$	90	1	2C2a, 2C2b	Y2 Summer Test 1
12	$\frac{1}{3}$ of $15 = \square$	5	1	2F1a	Y2 Summer Test 3
13	$378 + 10 = \square$	388	1	3N2b	Y3 Autumn Test 3
14	$524 - 7 = \square$	517	1	3C1	Y3 Autumn Test 2
15	$\square = 721 + 70$	791	1	3C1	Y3 Autumn Test 3
16	$340 + 564 = \square$	904	1	3C2	Y3 Autumn Test 4
17	$522 - 263 = \square$	259	1	3C2	Y3 Summer Test 1
18	$\square \div 4 = 9$	36	1	3C8	Y3 Spring Test 4, Y3 Summer Test 6
19	$\square + 356 = 752$	396	1	3C4	Y3 Autumn Test 4, Y3 Summer Test 6
20	$8 \times 9 = \square$	72	1	3C6	Y3 Spring Test 3, Y3 Spring Test 5
21	$\frac{8}{10} - \frac{6}{10} = \square$	$\frac{2}{10}$	1	3F1a	Y3 Autumn Test 5, Y3 Spring Test 1
22	$\square = 51 \times 8$	408	1	3C7	Y3 Spring Test 6, Y3 Summer Test 5
23	$\frac{1}{8} + \frac{4}{8} = \square$	$\frac{5}{8}$	1	3F4	Y3 Autumn Test 5
24	$\frac{1}{5}$ of $25 = \square$	5	1	3F1b	Y3 Summer Test 3
25	$\square - 143 = 277$	420	1	3C4	Y3 Summer Test 1, Y3 Summer Test 6

Summer Test 1

1 $9 - 6 =$ ⬜

2 $8 - $ ⬜ $= 7$

3 $5 \times 11 =$ ⬜

4 $16 - 7 =$ ⬜

5 $50 - 10 - 10 =$ ⬜

6 $95 - 8 =$ ⬜

7 $18 \div 2 =$ ⬜

8 $48 - 20 =$ ⬜

9 $6 + 6 + 2 =$ ⬜

10 $\frac{1}{2}$ of $18 =$ ⬜

11   ⬜ $= 64 + 26$

12 $\frac{1}{3}$ of $15 =$ ⬜

13 $378 + 10 =$ ⬜

14 $524 - 7 =$ ⬜

Arithmetic Practice Tests Set B Year 3 © Rising Stars UK Ltd 2017

Summer Test 1 (continued)

15 $\boxed{} = 721 + 70$

16 $340 + 564 = \boxed{}$

17 $522 - 263 = \boxed{}$

18 $\boxed{} \div 4 = 9$

19 $\boxed{} + 356 = 752$

20 $8 \times 9 = \boxed{}$

21 $\dfrac{8}{10} - \dfrac{6}{10} = \boxed{}$

22 $\boxed{} = 51 \times 8$

23 $\dfrac{1}{8} + \dfrac{4}{8} = \boxed{}$

24 $\dfrac{1}{5}$ of $25 = \boxed{}$

25 $\boxed{} - 143 = 277$

Total marks	/25

How well did you do?
Colour the numbers of the questions you got correct.

+	9	11	13	15	16	19	23			
−	1	2	4	5	6	8	14	17	21	25
x	3	20	22							
÷	7	18								
Fractions	10	12	21	23	24					
Missing numbers	2	18	19	25						

Summer Test 2

Teacher guidance

25 minutes

Skills and knowledge covered in this test:

- Count from 0 in multiples of 4, 8, 50 and 100 [3N1b]
- Find 10 or 100 more or less than a given number [3N2b]
- Add and subtract mentally [3C1]
- Add and subtract using formal written methods of columnar addition and subtraction [3C2]
- Solve addition and subtraction problems including missing numbers [3C4]
- Recall multiplication and division facts for the 3, 4 and 8 multiplication tables [3C6]
- Calculate multiplication and division statements mentally and using formal written methods [3C7]
- Solve multiplication and division problems including missing numbers [3C8]
- Count up and down in tenths [3F1a]
- Find fractions of a discrete set of objects [3F1b]
- Add and subtract fractions with the same denominator [3F4]

Focus activity: Fractions, division and equivalent fractions

3F1c, 3F2

You will need: strips of plain paper 24 cm long, or strips of 2 cm squared paper 12 squares long, counters or cubes.

 Step 1 Give each child several strips of paper. Place one strip on the table and label it 1. Fold the next strip in half and label each half. When you divide by two, each equal part is called a half, $\frac{1}{2}$. So $1 \div 2 = \frac{1}{2}$.

Step 2 Fold and label the paper strips to make a fraction wall up to tenths. Children may need support with accurate folding and labelling. Link each strip to the matching division:

$1 \div 2 = \frac{1}{2}$

$1 \div 3 = \frac{1}{3}$

$1 \div 4 = \frac{1}{4}$

$1 \div 5 = \frac{1}{5}$

 Step 3 Focus on the fold line for $\frac{1}{2}$. Look up and down the fraction wall to find equivalent fractions that are the same size. Line up the relevant paper strips next to each other to check that $\frac{1}{2} = \frac{2}{4} = \frac{3}{6} = \frac{4}{8} = \frac{5}{10}$.

 Step 4 Challenge children to find other sets of equivalent fractions, e.g. $\frac{1}{3} = \frac{2}{6} = \frac{3}{9}$. Challenge children to use the patterns in the numbers to predict the next fraction in the sequence.

Qu. No.	Question	Answer	Mark	Domain ref.	Focus activity
1	$8 + 4 = \square$	12	1	1C1	Y1 Summer Test 2, Y1 Summer Test 4
2	$9 - \square = 3$	6	1	1C4	Y1 Spring Test 1, Y1 Spring Test 5, Y1 Summer Test 4, Y1 Summer Test 6
3	$3 \times 11 = \square$	33	1	3C6	Y3 Spring Test 3, Y3 Spring Test 5
4	$8 \times 2 = \square$	16	1	2C6	Y2 Spring Test 1, Y2 Spring Test 2
5	$13 - 7 = \square$	6	1	2C1	Y1 Summer Test 3, Y1 Summer Test 4
6	$23 + 30 = \square$	53	1	2C2a, 2C2b	Y2 Autumn Test 5
7	$80 + 10 + 10 = \square$	100	1	2N1	Y2 Autumn Test 5
8	$\frac{3}{4}$ of $24 = \square$	18	1	2F1a	Y2 Summer Test 3
9	$85 + 8 = \square$	93	1	2C2a, 2C2b	Y2 Autumn Test 1
10	$\square = 32 \div 4$	8	1	3C6	Y3 Spring Test 5
11	$249 + 2 = \square$	251	1	3C1	Y3 Autumn Test 2
12	$8 + 6 + 7 = \square$	21	1	2C2a, 2C2b	Y2 Autumn Test 4
13	$\frac{1}{4}$ of $44 = \square$	11	1	2F1a	Y2 Summer Test 3
14	$76 - 47 = \square$	29	1	2C2a, 2C2b	Y2 Summer Test 2
15	$436 + 400 = \square$	836	1	3C1	Y3 Autumn Test 3
16	$8 \times 3 = \square$	24	1	3C6	Y3 Spring Test 3, Y3 Spring Test 5
17	$\square = 287 + 298$	585	1	3C2	Y3 Autumn Test 4
18	$632 - 100 = \square$	532	1	3N2b	Y3 Autumn Test 3
19	$535 - 266 = \square$	269	1	3C2	Y3 Summer Test 1
20	$\frac{6}{10} - \frac{3}{10} = \square$	$\frac{3}{10}$	1	3F1a	Y3 Autumn Test 5, Y3 Spring Test 1
21	$45 \div \square = 5$	9	1	3C8	Y3 Spring Test 4, Y3 Summer Test 6
22	$603 - \square = 178$	425	1	3C4	Y3 Summer Test 1, Y3 Summer Test 6
23	$55 \times 5 = \square$	275	1	3C7	Y3 Spring Test 6, Y3 Summer Test 5
24	$\square = \frac{1}{3} + \frac{1}{3}$	$\frac{2}{3}$	1	3F4	Y3 Autumn Test 5
25	$\frac{4}{5}$ of $50 = \square$	40	1	3F1b	Y3 Autumn Test 6, Y3 Summer Test 3

Summer Test 2

Name: .... **Class:** .... **Date:** ....

1 $8 + 4 =$ ☐

2 $9 - \boxed{} = 3$

3 $3 \times 11 =$ ☐

4 $8 \times 2 =$ ☐

5 $13 - 7 =$ ☐

6 $23 + 30 =$ ☐

7 $80 + 10 + 10 =$ ☐

8 $\frac{3}{4}$ of $24 =$ ☐

9 $85 + 8 =$ ☐

10 $\boxed{} = 32 \div 4$

11 $249 + 2 =$ ☐

12 $8 + 6 + 7 =$ ☐

13 $\frac{1}{4}$ of $44 =$ ☐

14 $76 - 47 =$ ☐

Summer Test 2 (continued)

15 $436 + 400 = \boxed{}$

16 $8 \times 3 = \boxed{}$

17 $\boxed{} = 287 + 298$

18 $632 - 100 = \boxed{}$

19 $535 - 266 = \boxed{}$

20 $\dfrac{6}{10} - \dfrac{3}{10} = \boxed{}$

21 $45 \div \boxed{} = 5$

22 $603 - \boxed{} = 178$

23 $55 \times 5 = \boxed{}$

24 $\boxed{} = \dfrac{1}{3} + \dfrac{1}{3}$

25 $\dfrac{4}{5}$ of $50 = \boxed{}$

Total marks	/25

How well did you do?
Colour the numbers of the
questions you got correct.

+	1	6	7	9	11	12	15	17	24
−	2	5		14	18	19	20	22	
×	3	4	16	23					
÷	10			21					
Fractions	8	13	20	24	25				
Missing numbers	2	21	22						

Summer Test 3

Teacher guidance

25 minutes

Skills and knowledge covered in this test:

- Count from 0 in multiples of 4, 8, 50 and 100 [3N1b]
- Find 10 or 100 more or less than a given number [3N2b]
- Add and subtract mentally [3C1]
- Add and subtract using formal written methods of columnar addition and subtraction [3C2]
- Solve addition and subtraction problems including missing numbers [3C4]
- Recall multiplication and division facts for the 3, 4 and 8 multiplication tables [3C6]

- Calculate multiplication and division statements mentally and using formal written methods [3C7]
- Solve multiplication and division problems including missing numbers [3C8]
- Count up and down in tenths [3F1a]
- Find fractions of a discrete set of objects [3F1b]
- Add and subtract fractions with the same denominator [3F4]

Focus activity: Fractions of a quantity

3F1b, 3F1c

You will need: strips of plain paper 24 cm long, or strips of 2 cm squared paper 12 squares long, counters or cubes.

 Give children paper strips to create a fraction wall, as in the activity for the Summer Test 2.

 Give children 24 counters or cubes and ask them to use their fraction wall to find $\frac{1}{2}$, $\frac{1}{3}$, $\frac{1}{4}$, $\frac{1}{6}$ and $\frac{1}{8}$ of 24. Children sort the counters onto a strip, e.g. placing 24 counters into sections of the thirds fraction strip to find that each $\frac{1}{3}$ should have eight counters on it. Children should record their findings in the format: $\frac{1}{3}$ of 24 = 8.

 Ask children to explain why you did not ask them to find $\frac{1}{5}$, $\frac{1}{7}$, $\frac{1}{9}$ or $\frac{1}{10}$ of 24.

 Challenge children to find some non-unit fractions of 24, for example $\frac{2}{3}$, $\frac{3}{4}$, $\frac{2}{6}$, $\frac{5}{8}$ and so on.

 Give children six more counters, 30 altogether. Challenge them to find at least ten different fractions of 30, recording their fractions as above.

Qu. No.	Question	Answer	Mark	Domain ref.	Focus activity
1	$9 - 1 = \square$	8	1	1C1	Y1 Autumn Test 4, Y1 Summer Test 4
2	$7 - \square = 5$	2	1	1C4	Y1 Spring Test 1, Y1 Spring Test 5, Y1 Summer Test 4, Y1 Summer Test 6
3	$\square = 12 \div 2$	6	1	2C6	Y2 Spring Test 3, Y2 Spring Test 4, Y2 Spring Test 5, Y2 Spring Test 6
4	$7 \times 5 = \square$	35	1	2C6	Y2 Spring Test 1, Y2 Spring Test 2
5	$18 - 4 = \square$	14	1	2C1	Y1 Summer Test 3, Y1 Summer Test 4
6	$50 + 10 + 10 = \square$	70	1	2N1	Y2 Autumn Test 5
7	$70 - 7 = \square$	63	1	2C2a, 2C2b	Y2 Autumn Test 2
8	$484 + 100 = \square$	584	1	3N2b	Y3 Autumn Test 3
9	$53 - \square = 30$	23	1	2C4	Y2 Summer Test 2, Y2 Summer Test 5
10	$58 + 31 = \square$	89	1	2C2a, 2C2b	Y2 Summer Test 1
11	$9 + 4 + 5 = \square$	18	1	2C2a, 2C2b	Y2 Autumn Test 4
12	$\frac{1}{2}$ of $26 = \square$	13	1	2F1a	Y2 Summer Test 3
13	$887 + 7 = \square$	894	1	3C1	Y3 Autumn Test 2
14	$\square = 618 + 80$	698	1	3C1	Y3 Autumn Test 3
15	$642 - 300 = \square$	342	1	3C1	Y3 Autumn Test 3
16	$3 \times 9 = \square$	27	1	3C6	Y3 Spring Test 3, Y3 Spring Test 5
17	$183 + 542 = \square$	725	1	3C2	Y3 Autumn Test 4
18	$\square = \frac{3}{10} + \frac{2}{10}$	$\frac{5}{10}$	1	3F1a	Y3 Autumn Test 5, Y3 Spring Test 1
19	$363 - 175 = \square$	188	1	3C2	Y3 Summer Test 1
20	$\frac{2}{9} + \frac{5}{9} = \square$	$\frac{7}{9}$	1	3F4	Y3 Autumn Test 5
21	$8 \times 8 = \square$	64	1	3C6	Y3 Spring Test 5
22	$\square \times 3 = 18$	6	1	3C8	Y3 Spring Test 4, Y3 Summer Test 6
23	$\frac{5}{8}$ of $24 = \square$	15	1	3F1b	Y3 Autumn Test 6, Y3 Summer Test 3
24	$\square - 256 = 645$	901	1	3C4	Y3 Summer Test 1, Y3 Summer Test 6
25	$43 \times 8 = \square$	344	1	3C7	Y3 Spring Test 6, Y3 Summer Test 5

Summer Test 3

Name: .... Class: .... Date: ....

1 $9 - 1 = \boxed{}$

2 $7 - \boxed{} = 5$

3 $\boxed{} = 12 \div 2$

4 $7 \times 5 = \boxed{}$

5 $18 - 4 = \boxed{}$

6 $50 + 10 + 10 = \boxed{}$

7 $70 - 7 = \boxed{}$

8 $484 + 100 = \boxed{}$

9 $53 - \boxed{} = 30$

10 $58 + 31 = \boxed{}$

11 $9 + 4 + 5 = \boxed{}$

12 $\frac{1}{2}$ of $26 = \boxed{}$

13 $887 + 7 = \boxed{}$

14 $\boxed{} = 618 + 80$

Arithmetic Practice Tests Set B Year 3 © Rising Stars UK Ltd 2017

Summer Test 3 (continued)

15 $642 - 300 = \boxed{}$

16 $3 \times 9 = \boxed{}$

17 $183 + 542 = \boxed{}$

18 $\boxed{} = \frac{3}{10} + \frac{2}{10}$

19 $363 - 175 = \boxed{}$

20 $\frac{2}{9} + \frac{5}{9} = \boxed{}$

21 $8 \times 8 = \boxed{}$

22 $\boxed{} \times 3 = 18$

23 $\frac{5}{8}$ of $24 = \boxed{}$

24 $\boxed{} - 256 = 645$

25 $43 \times 8 = \boxed{}$

Total marks	/25

How well did you do?
Colour the numbers of the questions you got correct.

+	6	8	10	11	13	17	18	20
−	1	2	5	7	9	15	19	24
×	4	16	21	22	25			
÷	3							
Fractions	12	14	18	20	23			
Missing numbers	2	9	22	24				

Summer Test 4

Teacher guidance

25 minutes

Skills and knowledge covered in this test

- Count from 0 in multiples of 4, 8, 50 and 100 [3N1b]
- Find 10 or 100 more or less than a given number [3N2b]
- Add and subtract mentally [3C1]
- Add and subtract using formal written methods of columnar addition and subtraction [3C2]
- Solve addition and subtraction problems including missing numbers [3C4]
- Recall multiplication and division facts for the 3, 4 and 8 multiplication tables [3C6]
- Calculate multiplication and division statements mentally and using formal written methods [3C7]
- Solve multiplication and division problems including missing numbers [3C8]
- Count up and down in tenths [3F1a]
- Find fractions of a discrete set of objects [3F1b]
- Add and subtract fractions with the same denominator [3F4]

Focus activity: Mental or written methods?

3C1, 3C2

You will need: 0–9 digit cards.

 Step 1 Explain that, when solving calculations, mental methods are generally faster than written methods, so it is always best to see if you can use a mental method before using a standard written method.

 Step 2 Tell children that they should first look at the numbers involved. If any number is close to a multiple of hundreds or tens, it could be better to work mentally.

Addition: 398 + 174. 398 is close to 400. 400 + 174 = 574. This is 2 too many because 400 is 2 more than 398, so we need to subtract 2. So 398 + 174 = 574 – 2 = 572.

Addition: 359 + 107. 107 is close to 100, so add 100 then 7. 359 + 100 + 7 = 459 + 7 = 466.

Subtraction: 463 – 197. 197 is close to 200, so subtract 200. This is 3 too many because 200 is 3 more than 197 so we need to add back 3. 463 – 197 = 463 – 200 + 3 = 263 + 3 = 266.

Subtraction: 463 – 204. 204 is close to 200, so subtract the 200 then the 4. 463 – 200 – 4 = 263 – 4 = 259.

 Step 3 Shuffle a set of digit cards. Lay out six cards to make two 3-digit numbers. Look at the numbers and decide whether to add and subtract and whether to use a mental or a written method. Record accordingly.

Qu. No.	Question	Answer	Mark	Domain ref.	Focus activity
1	$5 - 4 = \square$	1	1	1C1	Y1 Autumn Test 4, Y1 Summer Test 4
2	$\square = 2 \times 10$	20	1	2C6	Y2 Spring Test 1, Y2 Spring Test 2
3	$9 - \square = 2$	7	1	1C4	Y1 Spring Test 1, Y1 Spring Test 5, Y1 Summer Test 4, Y1 Summer Test 6
4	$3 + 7 + 8 = \square$	18	1	2C2a, 2C2b	Y2 Autumn Test 4
5	$14 - 2 = \square$	12	1	2C1	Y1 Summer Test 3, Y1 Summer Test 4
6	$\frac{1}{4}$ of $4 = \square$	1	1	2F1a	Y2 Summer Test 3
7	$55 \div 5 = \square$	11	1	2C6	Y2 Spring Test 3, Y1 Spring Test 4, Y1 Spring Test 5, Y1 Spring Test 6
8	$100 - 10 - 10 = \square$	80	1	2N1	Y3 Autumn Test 3
9	$92 + 6 = \square$	98	1	2C2a, 2C2b	Y2 Autumn Test 1
10	$43 + 40 = \square$	83	1	2C2a, 2C2b	Y2 Autumn Test 5
11	$62 - 28 = \square$	34	1	2C2a, 2C2b	Y2 Summer Test 1
12	$932 - 10 = \square$	922	1	3N2b	Y3 Autumn Test 3
13	$\square = 7 \div 10$	0.7	1	3F1a	Y3 Spring Test 1
14	$4 \times 8 = \square$	32	1	3C6	Y3 Spring Test 3, Y3 Spring Test 5
15	$654 - 6 = \square$	648	1	3C1	Y3 Autumn Test 2
16	$936 - 500 = \square$	436	1	3C1	Y3 Autumn Test 3
17	$8 \times 6 = \square$	48	1	3C6	Y3 Spring Test 5
18	$755 + 178 = \square$	933	1	3C2	Y3 Autumn Test 4
19	$732 - 427 = \square$	305	1	3C2	Y3 Summer Test 1
20	$\frac{5}{10} + \frac{4}{10} = \square$	$\frac{9}{10}$	1	3F1a	Y3 Autumn Test 5, Y3 Spring Test 1
21	$\square = \frac{5}{9} - \frac{3}{9}$	$\frac{2}{9}$	1	3F4	Y3 Autumn Test 5
22	$647 - \square = 472$	175	1	3C4	Y3 Summer Test 1, Y3 Summer Test 6
23	$\frac{2}{3}$ of $21 = \square$	14	1	3F1b	Y3 Autumn Test 6, Y3 Summer Test 3
24	$\square \div 8 = 9$	72	1	3C8	Y3 Spring Test 4, Y3 Summer Test 6
25	$38 \times 3 = \square$	114	1	3C7	Y3 Spring Test 6, Y3 Summer Test 5

Summer Test 4

Name: .... **Class:** .... **Date:** ....

1 $5 - 4 = \boxed{}$

2 $\boxed{} = 2 \times 10$

3 $9 - \boxed{} = 2$

4 $3 + 7 + 8 = \boxed{}$

5 $14 - 2 = \boxed{}$

6 $\frac{1}{4}$ of $4 = \boxed{}$

7 $55 \div 5 = \boxed{}$

8 $100 - 10 - 10 = \boxed{}$

9 $92 + 6 = \boxed{}$

10 $43 + 40 = \boxed{}$

11 $62 - 28 = \boxed{}$

12 $932 - 10 = \boxed{}$

13 $\boxed{} = 7 \div 10$

14 $4 \times 8 = \boxed{}$

Summer Test 4 (continued)

15 $654 - 6 = \boxed{}$

16 $936 - 500 = \boxed{}$

17 $8 \times 6 = \boxed{}$

18 $755 + 178 = \boxed{}$

19 $732 - 427 = \boxed{}$

20 $\dfrac{5}{10} + \dfrac{4}{10} = \boxed{}$

21 $\boxed{} = \dfrac{5}{9} - \dfrac{3}{9}$

22 $647 - \boxed{} = 472$

23 $\dfrac{2}{3}$ of $21 = \boxed{}$

24 $\boxed{} \div 8 = 9$

25 $38 \times 3 = \boxed{}$

Total marks | **/25**

How well did you do?
Colour the numbers of the questions you got correct.

+		4	9	10	18	20						
−		1	3	5	8	11	12	15	16	19	21	22
×		2	14	17	25							
÷			7			24						
Fractions		6	13	20	21	23						
Missing numbers		3	22	24								

Arithmetic Practice Tests Set B Year 3 © Rising Stars UK Ltd 2017

Summer Test 5

Teacher guidance

Skills and knowledge covered in this test:

- Count from 0 in multiples of 4, 8, 50 and 100 [3N1b]
- Find 10 or 100 more or less than a given number [3N2b]
- Add and subtract mentally [3C1]
- Add and subtract using formal written methods of columnar addition and subtraction [3C2]
- Solve addition and subtraction problems including missing numbers [3C4]
- Recall multiplication and division facts for the 3, 4 and 8 multiplication tables [3C6]
- Calculate multiplication and division statements mentally and using formal written methods [3C7]
- Solve multiplication and division problems including missing numbers [3C8]
- Count up and down in tenths [3F1a]
- Find fractions of a discrete set of objects [3F1b]
- Add and subtract fractions with the same denominator [3F4]

Focus activity: Written method for 2-digit numbers multiplied by a single digit

3C7

You will need: digit cards 1–5.

 Step 1 Draw a rectangle to represent the array for a multiplication, e.g. 27×5. Partition the 2-digit number into tens and ones. Label the rectangle accordingly.

$\times$	20	7
5	100	35

$100 + 35 = 135$

 Step 2 Record the expanded written method alongside the grid method. Highlight the 5×20 and the 5×7, exploring how each product is recorded and then how each column is added.

```
    27          27
  × 5         × 5
  ----        ----
    35         135
  100            3
  ----
  135
```

 Step 3 Then move on to the short written method. Again highlight how the products of 5×20 and 5×7 are recorded and where we write any numbers that we exchange.

 Step 4 Give children digit cards 1, 2, 3, 4, 5 and 8. Children arrange any three of the six cards into a 2-digit × single-digit multiplication using the written method. Challenge children to find the largest and smallest products. Encourage children to draw rectangles or use apparatus for support. Recording using the standard written layout will help children to compare products and identify their largest and smallest values.

Qu. No.	Question	Answer	Mark	Domain ref	Focus activity
1	$6 + 5 = \square$	11	1	1C1	Y1 Summer Test 2, Y1 Summer Test 4
2	$12 - 6 = \square$	6	1	2C1	Y1 Summer Test 3, Y1 Summer Test 4
3	$5 \times 5 = \square$	25	1	2C6	Y2 Spring Test 1, Y2 Spring Test 2
4	$8 - \square = 1$	7	1	1C4	Y1 Spring Test 1, Y1 Spring Test 5, Y1 Summer Test 4, Y1 Summer Test 6
5	$\frac{1}{2}$ of 20 $= \square$	10	1	2F1a	Y2 Summer Test 3
6	$60 + 10 + 10 = \square$	80	1	2N1	Y2 Autumn Test 5
7	$4 \times 11 = \square$	44	1	3C6	Y3 Spring Test 5
8	$\frac{3}{4}$ of 44 $= \square$	33	1	2F1a	Y2 Summer Test 3
9	$\frac{7}{10} + \frac{2}{10} = \square$	$\frac{9}{10}$	1	3F1a	Y3 Autumn Test 5, Y3 Spring Test 1
10	$\square = 32 + 4$	36	1	2C2a, 2C2b	Y2 Autumn Test 1
11	$14 \div 2 = \square$	7	1	2C6	Y2 Spring Test 3, Y2 Spring Test 4, Y2 Spring Test 5, Y2 Spring Test 6
12	$93 - 24 = \square$	69	1	2C2a, 2C2b	Y2 Summer Test 2
13	$5 + 9 + 3 = \square$	17	1	2C2a, 2C2b	Y2 Autumn Test 4
14	$68 + 20 = \square$	88	1	2C2a, 2C2b	Y2 Autumn Test 5
15	$8 \times \square = 88$	11	1	3C8	Y3 Spring Test 4, Y3 Summer Test 6
16	$638 - 100 = \square$	538	1	3N2b	Y3 Autumn Test 3
17	$\square = \frac{4}{5} - \frac{1}{5}$	$\frac{3}{5}$	1	3F4	Y3 Autumn Test 5
18	$37 \times 8 = \square$	296	1	3C7	Y3 Spring Test 6, Y3 Summer Test 5
19	$504 + 6 = \square$	510	1	3C1	Y3 Autumn Test 2
20	$\square = 463 + 267$	730	1	3C2	Y3 Autumn Test 4
21	$\frac{1}{8}$ of 32 $= \square$	4	1	3F1b	Y3 Summer Test 3
22	$640 - 354 = \square$	286	1	3C2	Y3 Summer Test 1
23	$8 \times \square = 72$	9	1	3C8	Y3 Spring Test 4, Y3 Summer Test 6
24	$\square + 547 = 781$	234	1	3C4	Y3 Autumn Test 4, Y3 Summer Test 6
25	$83 \times 4 = \square$	332	1	3C7	Y3 Spring Test 6, Y3 Summer Test 5

Summer Test 5

Name: ....   Class: ....   Date: ....

1 $6 + 5 =$ ☐

2 $12 - 6 =$ ☐

3 $5 \times 5 =$ ☐

4 $8 - $ ☐ $= 1$

5 $\frac{1}{2}$ of $20 =$ ☐

6 $60 + 10 + 10 =$ ☐

7 $4 \times 11 =$ ☐

8 $\frac{3}{4}$ of $44 =$ ☐

9 $\frac{7}{10} + \frac{2}{10} =$ ☐

10 ☐ $= 32 + 4$

11 $14 \div 2 =$ ☐

12 $93 - 24 =$ ☐

13 $5 + 9 + 3 =$ ☐

14 $68 + 20 =$ ☐

Arithmetic Practice Tests Set B Year 3 © Rising Stars UK Ltd 2017

Summer Test 5 (continued)

15 $8 \times \boxed{} = 88$

16 $638 - 100 = \boxed{}$

17 $\boxed{} = \frac{4}{5} - \frac{1}{5}$

18 $37 \times 8 = \boxed{}$

19 $504 + 6 = \boxed{}$

20 $\boxed{} = 463 + 267$

21 $\frac{1}{8}$ of $32 = \boxed{}$

22 $640 - 354 = \boxed{}$

23 $8 \times \boxed{} = 72$

24 $\boxed{} + 547 = 781$

25 $83 \times 4 = \boxed{}$

Total marks	/25

How well did you do?
Colour the numbers of the questions you got correct.

+		1	6	9	10	13	14	19	20	24
−		2	4	12	16	17	22			
×		3	7	15	18	23	25			
÷			11			21				
Fractions		5	8	9	17		21			
Missing numbers		4	15	23	24					

Summer Test 6

Teacher guidance

25 minutes

Skills and knowledge covered in this test

- Count from 0 in multiples of 4, 8, 50 and 100 [3N1b]
- Find 10 or 100 more or less than a given number [3N2b]
- Add and subtract mentally [3C1]
- Add and subtract using formal written methods of columnar addition and subtraction [3C2]
- Solve addition and subtraction problems including missing numbers [3C4]
- Recall multiplication and division facts for the 3, 4 and 8 multiplication tables [3C6]

- Calculate multiplication and division statements mentally and using formal written methods [3C7]
- Solve multiplication and division problems including missing numbers [3C8]
- Count up and down in tenths [3F1a]
- Find fractions of a discrete set of objects [3F1b]
- Add and subtract fractions with the same denominator [3F4]

Focus activity: Derived facts

3C4, 3C8

Step 1 Tell children that any addition, subtraction, multiplication or division fact can be used to make other facts.

Step 2 Demonstrate this. First choose a number fact, e.g. $6 + 4 = 10$. Double it: $12 + 8 = 20$; halve it: $3 + 2 = 5$; make it 10 times bigger or 10 times smaller: $60 + 40 = 100$; or do something else. Ask children to make other suggestions.

Step 3 Revise commutativity: in addition and multiplication, numbers can be added or multiplied in any order and the answer will always be the same, e.g. $2 + 3 = 3 + 2$ and $2 \times 3 = 3 \times 2$. Next revise associativity: in addition and multiplication, it doesn't matter how we group the numbers, the answer will always be the same, e.g. $(2 + 3) + 4 = 2 + (3 + 4)$ and $(2 \times 3) \times 4 = 2 \times (3 \times 4)$. Finally, revise fact families, e.g. $2 \times 3 = 6$, $3 \times 2 = 6$, $6 = 2 \times 3$, $6 = 3 \times 2$, $6 \div 2 = 3$, $6 \div 3 = 2$, $2 = 6 \div 3$, $3 = 6 \div 2$.

Step 4 Give children a new fact and challenge them to use it to make new, derived facts. After five to ten minutes, collect the derived facts and record them on the board in a spider diagram. Challenge each child to add a new fact to the spider diagram, ensuring children are able to explain how they derived it from the original.

Qu. No.	Question	Answer	Mark	Domain ref.	Focus activity
1	$8 + 6 = \square$	14	1	1C1	Y1 Summer Test 2, Y1 Summer Test 4
2	$6 - \square = 3$	3	1	1C4	Y1 Spring Test 1, Y1 Spring Test 5, Y1 Summer Test 4, Y1 Summer Test 6
3	$2 \times 5 = \square$	10	1	2C6	Y2 Spring Test 1, Y2 Spring Test 2
4	$19 - 5 = \square$	14	1	2C1	Y1 Summer Test 3, Y1 Summer Test 4
5	$70 + 100 = \square$	170	1	3N2b	Y2 Autumn Test 5
6	$70 \div 10 = \square$	7	1	2C6	Y2 Spring Test 3, Y2 Spring Test 4, Y2 Spring Test 5, Y2 Spring Test 6
7	$273 + 100 = \square$	373	1	3N2b	Y3 Autumn Test 3
8	$\square = 7 + 8 + 3$	18	1	2C2a, 2C2b	Y2 Autumn Test 4
9	$300 - 4 = \square$	296	1	3C1	Y3 Autumn Test 2
10	$342 + 500 = \square$	842	1	3C1	Y3 Autumn Test 3
11	$94 - 50 = \square$	44	1	2C2a, 2C2b	Y2 Autumn Test 5
12	$73 - 7 = \square$	66	1	2C2a, 2C2b	Y2 Autumn Test 2
13	$\frac{1}{4}$ of $48 = \square$	12	1	2F1a	Y2 Summer Test 3
14	$47 + 24 = \square$	71	1	2C2a, 2C2b	Y2 Summer Test 1
15	$3 \times 6 = \square$	18	1	3C6	Y3 Spring Test 3
16	$\frac{4}{10} - \frac{3}{10} = \square$	$\frac{1}{10}$	1	3F1a	Y3 Autumn Test 5, Y3 Spring Test 1
17	$\square \div 8 = 7$	56	1	3C8	Y3 Spring Test 4, Y3 Summer Test 6
18	$\square = 473 - 40$	433	1	3C1	Y3 Autumn Test 3
19	$648 + 265 = \square$	913	1	3C2	Y3 Autumn Test 4
20	$8 \times 9 = \square$	72	1	3C6	Y3 Spring Test 5
21	$\square = 735 - 537$	198	1	3C2	Y3 Summer Test 1
22	$\frac{5}{12} + \frac{3}{12} = \square$	$\frac{8}{12}$	1	3F4	Y3 Autumn Test 5
23	$457 + \square = 780$	323	1	3C4	Y3 Autumn Test 4, Y3 Summer Test 6
24	$53 \times 5 = \square$	265	1	3C7	Y3 Spring Test 6, Y3 Summer Test 5
25	$\frac{3}{5}$ of $20 = \square$	12	1	3F1b	Y3 Autumn Test 6, Y3 Summer Test 3

Summer Test 6

Name: .... Class: .... Date: ....

1 $8 + 6 = \boxed{}$

2 $6 - \boxed{} = 3$

3 $2 \times 5 = \boxed{}$

4 $19 - 5 = \boxed{}$

5 $70 + 100 = \boxed{}$

6 $70 \div 10 = \boxed{}$

7 $273 + 100 = \boxed{}$

8 $\boxed{} = 7 + 8 + 3$

9 $300 - 4 = \boxed{}$

10 $342 + 500 = \boxed{}$

11 $94 - 50 = \boxed{}$

12 $73 - 7 = \boxed{}$

13 $\frac{1}{4}$ of $48 = \boxed{}$

14 $47 + 24 = \boxed{}$

Summer Test 6 (continued)

15 $3 \times 6 = \boxed{}$

16 $\dfrac{4}{10} - \dfrac{3}{10} = \boxed{}$

17 $\boxed{} \div 8 = 7$

18 $\boxed{} = 473 - 40$

19 $648 + 265 = \boxed{}$

20 $8 \times 9 = \boxed{}$

21 $\boxed{} = 735 - 537$

22 $\dfrac{5}{12} + \dfrac{3}{12} = \boxed{}$

23 $457 + \boxed{} = 780$

24 $53 \times 5 = \boxed{}$

25 $\dfrac{3}{5}$ of $20 = \boxed{}$

Total marks	/25

How well did you do?
Colour the numbers of the questions you got correct.

+	1	5	7	8	10	14	19	22	23
−	2	4	9	11	12	16	21		
x	3	15	20	24					
÷	6		17						
Fractions	13	16	18	22	25				
Missing numbers	2	17	23						

Arithmetic Practice Tests Set B Year 3 © Rising Stars UK Ltd 2017